D1605815

Business Leaders:
WARREN BUFFETT

Bu$ine$$ Leader$
WARREN BUFFETT

Anne Janette Johnson

MORGAN
REYNOLDS

PUBLISHING

Greensboro, North Carolina

Bu$ine$$ Leader$:

Russell Simmons
Steve Jobs
Oprah Winfrey
Warren Buffett
Michael Dell
Ralph Lauren
Faces Behind Beauty

BUSINESS LEADERS: WARREN BUFFETT

Copyright © 2009 By Anne Janette Johnson

Library of Congress Cataloging-in-Publication Data

Johnson, Anne Janette, 1959-
  Business leaders : Warren Buffett / by Anne Janette Johnson.
     p. cm.
  Includes bibliographical references and index.
  ISBN-13: 978-1-59935-080-6
  ISBN-10: 1-59935-080-7
  1. Buffett, Warren. 2. Capitalists and financiers--United States--Biography.
I. Title.
HG172.B84J64 2007
332.6092--dc22
[B]
                                        2007045963

Printed in the United States of America

First Edition

Contents

Warren Buffett
(Courtesy of David Silverman/Getty Images)

ONE

The Boy Businessman

In the midst of the Great Depression, when the economy of the United States was in shambles and millions of Americans struggled with joblessness and poverty, six-year-old Warren Buffett found a way to make a tidy profit. During a family vacation to a lake area, the boy bought a six-pack of Coca-Cola for a quarter. He then walked around the lakefront, peddling individual bottles of Coke to sunbathers for five cents apiece. In short order, he was holding thirty cents—a 20 percent profit on his original investment. It was an auspicious start in business for a man who would one day be called the world's greatest investor.

Warren Edward Buffett was born August 30, 1930, in Omaha, Nebraska. Three generations of his family had prospered in the bustling city on the Missouri River, and the secrets of their success—hard work, frugality, and self-reliance—would serve him extraordinarily well.

Warren Buffett's great-grandfather, Sidney Buffett, had abandoned the life of a farmer on Long Island, New York, to go west. Arriving in Omaha in 1867, he quickly found work as a stagecoach driver.

Only a few years earlier, Omaha had been just a small frontier settlement, but now it was on the verge of a boom. The Pacific Railway Act, signed into law by President Abraham Lincoln in 1862, had authorized the construction of a railroad that would run from somewhere along the Missouri River to California. When linked to existing railroads farther east, the new line would connect the nation's two coasts. In 1863, Lincoln selected Omaha as the Missouri River terminal for the new transcontinental railroad, making the prairie town an important transportation and freight hub. Stockyards were built so that cattlemen could drive their herds to Omaha and ship

A view of Omaha, Nebraska, in 1947 *(Courtesy of Jerry Cooke/Time Life Pictures/Getty Images)*

them by rail to the eastern United States. People flocked to the growing town in search of jobs in construction, in railroad work, or in businesses that catered to railroad employees.

Sidney Buffett saw an opportunity. In 1869, the same year the transcontinental railroad was completed, he founded a small grocery store using money he had scrimped from his wages as a stagecoach driver. His timing could not have been better. Rapidly expanding Omaha had an appetite for the food he sold, including locally grown produce and wild game such as prairie hens and quail. Still, the business required long hours and hard work. But Sidney Buffett did not cut corners, and by constantly watching his pennies, he was able to turn a decent profit. Instead of spending his earnings on luxury items for himself or his family, he plunged them back into his business. He expanded his store to meet the growing demand in Omaha, hiring his two sons to help out.

One of the sons eventually quit. The other, Warren Buffett's grandfather Ernest, eventually took over the business. In 1915, Ernest Buffett moved the grocery from downtown Omaha to a location in the suburbs. There he prospered, and hewing to the Buffett tradition, saved and reinvested his profits in the business.

Even after he had become quite well-to-do, Ernest Buffett remained a strict taskmaster. He paid his workers minimal salaries and expected them to work long hours without complaint. Charlie Munger, who would later become Warren Buffett's friend and business partner, worked in the Buffett grocery for a time during the 1930s. In an interview with the *Omaha World-Herald*, Munger recalled that in addition to being paid just $2.00 for a twelve-hour shift—a meager wage even by the standards of the era—he had to reimburse Ernest Buffett two cents on each day's work. That was the portion of the Social Security tax that Buffett, as an employer, had to pay into the newly instituted federal program. According to Munger, Ernest Buffett detested Social Security, which paid retirement benefits for workers, as well as other government programs that gave handouts to the poor, viewing these programs as "the evil wedge of socialism."

Warren's father, Howard Buffett
(Library of Congress)

Ernest Buffett's son Howard—Warren's father—had no intention of working in the family business. Instead he attended the University of Nebraska at Lincoln, where he majored in journalism. During his senior year, while he was serving as the editor of the college newspaper, he met a fellow student named Leila Stahl. They married in Leila's hometown of West Point, Nebraska, on December 26, 1925.

A few years later the Buffetts welcomed their first child, a daughter they named Doris. Howard Buffett never realized his dream of working for a newspaper but instead took a position with an insurance company. By the time Warren was born in 1930, Howard Buffett had found a job selling stocks for the Union Street Bank in Omaha.

It was a difficult time for banks. The stock market crash of October 1929, which ushered in the Great Depression, also triggered a run on banks. Worried about the possibility of losing their savings, Americans rushed to their banks in droves and demanded to liquidate their accounts. Banks, which had

A crowd in the Wall Street district of Manhattan during the stock market crash of 1929 *(Courtesy of AP Images)*

invested a portion of the funds, did not have enough cash on hand to pay all the depositors who wished to close their accounts. Thousands of banks were forced out of business. In 1931, when Omaha's Union Street Bank became one of them, Howard Buffett suddenly found himself without a job.

With a wife and two young children to feed (another daughter, Roberta, or "Bertie," would soon join the family), Howard Buffett was forced to accept groceries on credit from his father. But he was determined to find a way to support his family on his own. Despite the dismal state of the stock market, he joined a friend in establishing a brokerage firm called Buffett, Sklenicka & Co.

Ernest Buffett scoffed at the venture, predicting that his son would fail. Worse, he actively discouraged his friends from investing with Buffett, Sklenicka & Co. Nevertheless, Howard Buffett managed to eke out a living on the scant commissions he received for investing his customers' money. Like millions of other American families, however, the Buffetts endured hardships and scuffled to make ends meet during the Great Depression.

It was during these tough times, when Warren Buffett was around five years old, that he resolved to become very rich someday. He did not forget that resolution, even after his father's brokerage firm began to prosper, easing the family's financial straits and making possible a family vacation. Buoyed by the success he experienced selling Cokes during that vacation, six-year-old Warren continued selling soft drinks, door-to-door, after his family returned to Omaha, continuing to make a profit of five cents on each six-pack he sold.

While many people would have been tempted to buy a bag of candy or attend a movie with the earned money, Warren was different. He kept his earnings and counted them carefully. At any given time, he knew exactly how much cash he had on hand. His most precious possession was a coin changer given to him by an aunt.

Numbers, patterns, and statistics fascinated Warren, and from a very young age he showed a remarkable gift for mathematics. He also had an uncanny ability to remember specific data—what some people call a photographic memory. A friend, Bob Russell, would read the names of cities to Warren from an almanac. Warren could recall the population of each city perfectly. "If I gave him ten cities, he'd hit every one," Russell said.

At seven Warren contracted a fever so serious that his doctors thought he might die. Terrified at the prospect of death, Warren lay in his sickbed and distracted himself by figuring sums and calculating how wealthy he would be—if he lived. Eventually his health returned, but he never lost his fear of death. Although raised by deeply religious parents, Warren found no solace in their Christian views of eternal life. He preferred to think about making money.

After school and on weekends, while other boys were playing sandlot baseball, Warren sold Cokes. He also delivered newspapers, and for a time he and a group of friends searched golf courses and driving ranges for lost golf balls, which they then sold. Warren, the leader of this enterprise, ranked the balls by brand name and value. He spent hours reading his favorite book, *One Thousand Ways to Make $1000.*

Gentle and good-humored, Warren had many friends. But he preferred to stay in familiar surroundings. Although of normal height and weight, he tended to avoid sports and rough games. His sisters Doris and Bertie fended off the occasional bully who might threaten him.

Warren loved his predictable life in Omaha—the friends, the easy hospitality of neighbors who welcomed him into their homes, the hours he spent memorizing major league baseball statistics, city populations, and the odds on horse races. Most of all, however, he loved going to his father's office building and watching the stock market ticker there. "I used to chart all kinds of stock, the more numbers the better," he recalled. He would watch the stock ticker as it relayed prices from Wall Street to Omaha, and then write the changes in stock prices on the blackboard in a downstairs office. Any information he deemed important he carried upstairs to his father, hour after hour. Howard Buffett adored his precocious son, whom he affectionately called "Fireball."

Warren greatly admired his father. "If I could be three quarters of the man he was, I'd be very pleased with myself," he said. "I just think he was the best human being I've known."

At the age of eleven, after spending many afternoons in his father's stock brokerage, Warren decided to invest his own money. He gathered all his savings and bought three shares in an energy company called Cities Service. He paid thirty-eight dollars per share. Warren watched anxiously while the stock price fell to twenty-seven dollars per share. When it rebounded to forty dollars, he sold the shares at a modest profit. Thereafter, Cities Service stock climbed rapidly, at one point selling for two-hundred dollars a share. If Warren had held on to his three shares, he would have reaped $486. From this experience he learned one of the most valuable lessons of his storied career: in the world of stocks, patience pays.

In 1942, not long after Warren had taken his first halting steps into stock market investment, local Republican leaders in Omaha convinced his father to run for Congress. No one really expected Howard Buffett to win the seat—least of all the Buffett family. The political newcomer's highly conservative views seemed out of step with the prevailing mood of the country. Howard Buffett railed against the domestic policies of President Franklin Delano Roosevelt, particularly Social Security and the New Deal legislation that had provided government-funded jobs to the unemployed during the recently ended Depression. Buffett, who had weathered the Depression through his own ability and hard work, believed that Roosevelt's policies discouraged Americans from being self-sufficient. But the Democratic president was immensely popular—he had already been elected to an unprecedented three terms in office—and he inspired loyalty to his party almost everywhere, including Omaha.

In the end, however, Howard Buffett underestimated his own popularity. "He was such an improbable candidate," his son recalled later, "that neither he nor his opponent took him seriously. On election night, he wrote out his concession statement, went to bed at nine o'clock and woke up the next morning to find he'd won."

The unexpected outcome dramatically changed the lives of the Buffetts. To the dismay of twelve-year-old Warren, the family had to move from his beloved Omaha so that his father could fulfill his duties in the U.S. House of Representatives. Because of a housing shortage in and around Washington, D.C., the Buffetts were unable to find a place to live within commuting distance of the nation's capital. While Leila, Doris, Warren, and Bertie settled into a home in Fredericksburg, Virginia, Howard Buffett rented a hotel room in Washington. He stayed there during the week, traveling to Fredericksburg to see his family only on weekends.

Warren greatly missed his father's daily presence, especially because he often found it hard to get along with his volatile mother. He was miserable in Fredericksburg: before the move he had been an honor student, but his grades fell off. "I told my parents I couldn't breathe," he said. "I told them not to worry about it, to get a good night's sleep themselves, and I'd just stand up all night." Given his past bouts of ill health, his worried parents eventually decided to send him back to Omaha to live with his grandfather.

Ernest Buffett promptly hired Warren part time to work in the grocery store. Warren did not particularly like the tasks he was given to do, such as hauling heavy crates and disposing of rotten produce. Still, he was back in the city he loved and learning how to run a successful business by watching his grandfather.

While dumping the rotten produce, Warren learned another lesson. As the grandson of the store's owner, he might have expected to be given easier duties and a better salary than the other workers, but his grandfather felt otherwise. To Ernest Buffett, family members should not be given special treatment. Assigning Warren an easier load would be akin to spoiling him. As much as he loved living in Omaha, young Warren greatly missed his father. He decided to rejoin his family in the fall of 1943. By this time the Buffetts had moved to a house in Washington, and Howard could come home every evening.

Warren Buffett was now ready to enter high school. He was also ready to start making serious money.

TWO

A Capital Education

Thirteen-year-old Warren Buffett gradually adjusted to his new life in Washington as the son of a congressman. He remained homesick for Omaha, but the opportunity to earn money in the nation's capital helped relieve the sting. This time the budding young capitalist concentrated on newspaper delivery.

Most newspaper carriers of the day rode small routes on bicycles, flinging papers to front porches and collecting subscription money once a month. When Warren began delivering the *Washington Post* in 1943, he did so in his typically ambitious way.

His father said Warren could deliver as many newspapers as he liked, so long as he kept up his grades. Warren accepted the challenge. He signed up for five full routes, most of them in huge apartment buildings downtown. Realizing that some

Newspaper boys preparing papers for delivery *(Library of Congress)*

readers preferred Washington's other morning paper, the *Washington Times-Herald,* he started delivering that too. Then he began to sell magazine subscriptions to his customers. He kept impeccable records, tracking the expiration dates of magazines by combing apartment hallways for discarded issues. He also worked with the elevator operators in his buildings. In exchange for free newspapers, they let him know when a customer planned to move. Warren would promptly visit the customer for a final subscription payment.

By the time he was a sophomore in high school, Warren was responsible for delivering five hundred newspapers a day. He charted the easiest and quickest way to get all the papers onto all the doorsteps. In the apartment buildings, he used staging areas on certain floors, dropping all the papers for several floors in stacks, and then quickly dispersing them to the customers on those floors. He learned that some apartment complexes had underground connecting passageways, and he used these to avoid bad weather. Customers could pay their bills at the front desk, saving him the time-consuming task of knocking on hundreds of doors.

His monthly earnings topped $175. At the time, the average adult in full-time work was making only about $215 a month.

Warren filled out and filed his own tax return. He still has on file in his office the first return he submitted, at age thirteen. On that return he deducted the cost of his bicycle as a business expense.

Like his father and grandfather before him, he was reluctant to spend his profits. The most modest clothing satisfied him. When he finally did make a purchase, his friends thought he had lost his mind. He bought forty acres of farmland in Nebraska for $1,200.

Not content with the money he earned from delivering newspapers and magazines, Buffett teamed up with a Woodrow Wilson High classmate, Donald Danly, in another venture. Though not particularly interested in business, Danly liked to tinker with broken equipment. He and Buffett combed Washington's arcades and secondhand stores, looking for broken pinball machines. Buffett bought the machines, Danly fixed them, and then the two boys leased them to barbershops throughout the city, delivering the machines in a 1938 Buick that Danly had repaired. The business began on a small scale, with one machine in one location. But Buffett and Danly soon expanded, giving their undertaking a name—Wilson Coin Operated Machine Company—and keeping accounts for customers, repairs, purchases, and travel expenses.

Every week the two high school students made the rounds of the barbershops, collecting the coins from the pinball machines. They gave half the profits to the shop owners and split the other half between them. Within a few months, each

Men gathered around a pinball machine in 1941 *(Library of Congress)*

boy was making fifty dollars a week after all the deductions for repairs, purchases, and gasoline.

In that era, grown men could make a living by leasing pinball machines, so Buffett and Danly had to pretend that they worked for some shadowy adult. "The barbershop operators were always pushing us to put in new machines, and we'd always tell them we'd take it up with the boss," Buffett said. "We pretended like we were the hired hands that were carrying machines around and counting money."

High school did not challenge Buffett academically. He made honor roll grades with plenty of time left over to conduct his businesses and to read books about the stock market, finance, and the principles of running a profitable company. His teachers, knowing his preoccupation with stocks, asked for tips. Occasionally, if he didn't like them, he offered bad advice on purpose. "I thought I would . . . terrorize them about their retirement," he recalled.

During his high school years, Buffett maintained the warm relationship he had always enjoyed with his father. But he began to form his own political philosophy, finding that he differed from his father in many respects. Howard Buffett was aggressively conservative. He opposed nearly all of Franklin Roosevelt's legislation and attacked Roosevelt's New Deal for "fastening the chains of political servitude around America's neck" in the form of high taxes and government giveaways. After the end of World War II in 1945, the Nebraska congressman opposed efforts by Roosevelt's successor, President Harry Truman, to finance the rebuilding of Europe. He believed fervently that money devoted to foreign aid should remain in the United States and that the country should isolate itself from world politics.

His father was a lifelong Republican, but gradually Warren Buffett gravitated to the Democratic Party. He thought the government should offer aid to the less fortunate, both at home and abroad. Unlike his father, he believed that the wealthy should pay more taxes so that the poor need not suffer the worst degrees of want. After the American use of nuclear weapons against Japan to end World War II, he concluded that the United States should not isolate itself from the rest of the world but instead should lead the way in promoting peaceful solutions to conflicts between other countries. Still, the political disagreements "didn't change my feelings about him."

In the spring of 1947, father and son finally had an open disagreement, but it was not about politics. During his four years in high school, Warren Buffett had earned $5,000 from his paper routes, had founded a full-fledged business, and was receiving rent from the farmer who was working the land he had bought in Nebraska. At sixteen he was earning the equivalent, in today's currency, of about $40,000. After graduating from high school, he planned to go straight to work for a bank or stock brokerage firm, believing that college tuition would be a waste of money. Howard Buffett disagreed. His son had already been accepted into the Wharton School of the University of Pennsylvania, considered one of the best business programs in the United States. Howard argued that Warren could not pass up the opportunity to attend such a prestigious institution, many of whose graduates landed executive positions in business and industry. Ultimately, the elder Buffett prevailed, and Warren agreed to attend Wharton in the fall.

In the meantime, his high school career ended on a high note. Among the 374 graduating members of Woodrow Wilson High's class of 1947, Warren Buffett ranked sixteenth— a particularly impressive achievement given his hectic outside schedule of business enterprises, self-directed reading, and stock speculation. The caption under his portrait in the yearbook noted: "Likes math . . . a future stockbroker."

The "future stockbroker" faced a difficult adjustment in the fall, when he traveled to Philadelphia to attend the Wharton School. Just seventeen, he found himself surrounded by older students—some of them veterans of World War II who were well into their twenties. Yet Buffett was well prepared for the Wharton curriculum. He already understood many of the business principles his professors introduced in their lectures, and sometimes he challenged their views. Because of his excellent memory, he could muster a wealth

The Wharton School of the University of Pennsylvania *(Courtesy of Nick Higham/Alamy)*

of evidence to support his arguments. He rarely studied for tests and later confessed that to get an "A" all he needed was a few hours of reading from the classroom text and a big bottle of Pepsi.

Buffett roomed with another Omaha native, Charles Peterson. Peterson did what he could to help his young roommate make friends. Though he had a good sense of humor and liked to play bridge, Buffett avoided typical college social gatherings such as parties or sporting events, and he did not date.

In his sophomore year at Wharton, Buffett pledged Alpha Sigma Phi fraternity and took rooms in the fraternity house. Fraternities offered more comfortable living arrangements and better food than could be found in dormitories and dining halls. They also offered more social opportunities. Gradually Buffett learned to be at ease in these situations.

Surrounded by students old enough to drink alcohol, he stuck strictly to Pepsi—he has been a lifetime devotee of soft drinks—and earned the admiration of his classmates for his dry, midwestern humor. But Buffett had been correct when he told his father that Wharton would not be a good fit for him. He missed Omaha. At the end of his second year in Philadelphia, he decided to finish his college education closer to home, at the University of Nebraska, Lincoln.

Back in Nebraska, Buffett structured his studies so that he could earn a bachelor's degree with just one more year of school. In addition to taking extra courses, he also supervised paperboys who delivered the *Lincoln Journal* in the farming counties around Nebraska's capital.

During the spring term, while he was taking six courses in business and finance, Buffett also returned to his youthful enterprise of selling used golf balls. This time he recruited youngsters to find the balls, which he sorted and sent to his best friend at Wharton to sell in Philadelphia. Between the newspaper job and the golf ball venture, as well as his previous enterprises and his farm, Buffett ended the summer of 1950 with a bachelor's degree from the University of Nebraska *and* a bank account containing $9,800. It was a significant sum for a nineteen-year-old full-time student to have accumulated while graduating early.

Buffett finally agreed with his father about the importance of higher learning. He applied to the graduate program at the prestigious Harvard Business School. "The interview in Chicago took about ten minutes," he recalled, "and they threw me back in the water." Buffett was stung by the rejection from Harvard, especially since his interviewer dismissed him so abruptly.

He was not out of options, however. He had read a book called *The Intelligent Investor* by the respected stock analyst Benjamin Graham. Graham, who ran his own Wall Street investment firm, also taught at the Columbia University graduate school of business in New York City. In hopes of studying with Graham, Buffett applied to Columbia. Characteristically, by the time Columbia notified him that he had been accepted, Buffett had read all of Graham's books.

After bidding farewell to his family in Omaha late in the summer of 1950, Buffett boarded a train for Manhattan. He was about to meet the man who would truly teach him how to become rich.

THREE

Ben's Bargains

ometimes teachers and students form bonds that last beyond the years of formal education. Occasionally a teacher will recognize a special student and develop a long-lasting partnership of ideas. The relationship between Warren Buffett and Benjamin Graham became just such a partnership.

Graham, fifty-six-years-old in 1950, had been investing in the stock market since the 1920s. During the 1930s, after the stock market crash of 1929 had nearly ruined his investment firm, Graham began to lecture and write about his particular investment philosophy, which came to be known as value investing. In 1934, at the height of the Depression, he and coauthor David Dodd published an important book on the subject. The book, *Security Analysis,* challenged the entire way people invested in stocks.

Benjamin Graham *(Courtesy of AP Images)*

According to Graham and Dodd, most investors put their money into stocks based not upon the quality of the business in which they were investing, but upon emotion and upon the way other people were investing their money. Graham and Dodd accused stockbrokers of having a herd mentality, following one another and panicking if stock prices did not rise quickly.

Security Analysis advocated studying the finances of individual businesses closely, in order to discover which ones had the best prospects for improvement over time or the most unused assets. Graham and Dodd favored bargains, or businesses in which the stock price was low, given the company assets and cash on hand. If a business had enough money to pay its shareholders more than the current price of the stock, the authors saw that business as a sound investment opportunity.

After his investment firm had recovered from the losses it sustained as a result of the stock market crash, Graham used his ideas about value investing to compile an impressive record on Wall Street. His methods often went against common practice and conventional wisdom. Graham criticized stockbrokers who watched daily stock prices for any change in value. He also dismissed stock tips as useless. While conventional wisdom held that stock prices always represented the full value of a company—and that if the prices were depressed, the company must be in trouble—Graham disagreed. A company's stock might be undervalued simply because that company was not well known among stockbrokers. Or the company might be in a depressed industry, but it might still have investments in other, more profitable enterprises. Through painstaking research, Graham would unearth the hidden value, the value that made the stock worth buying. He likened his bargain-hunting strategy to searching for a cigar butt that might have a few puffs left in it.

Using his mathematically based business-analysis techniques, Graham could find companies whose stock traded at one-third the value of the company's net working capital (its assets minus its liabilities). But the method required a great deal of work. A motivated, Graham-influenced investor needed to read dozens or even hundreds of annual reports issued by publicly traded businesses in order to find a rare undervalued gem. Public companies, or those that trade on Wall Street, must by law submit annual reports to their investors. They also might issue quarterly or even monthly earnings reports. With the patience of an archaeologist sifting tons of earth for a few artifacts, Graham studied these financial records, looking line-by-line for hidden value.

A photo of Buffett from the 1950s

Warren Buffett liked Graham's emphasis on carefully using the numbers to evaluate a company and its stock. He also agreed with the underlying premises of Graham's value investing: an investor should choose the right company and then have the patience to let it grow. The tipsters and day traders might make a quick profit one day, but they were likely to lose it the next.

Years later, summing up Graham's approach, Buffett explained:

> Ben just says, look at a stock not as some thing that wiggles around or is quoted in the paper every day or is up there on a ticker. Look at it as a piece of a business. Figure out what the business is worth. If you can't figure out what the business is worth, you have got no business buying the stock. . . . I had never thought of it that way. And so I started looking at businesses instead of stock charts and volume and all that kind of thing. And it was amazing, what kind of an edge that gave me.

When they met at Columbia University in the fall of 1950, the venerable Graham and his bright young pupil from Omaha liked each other immediately. The other students enrolled in Graham's graduate-level classes were much older than Buffett. Many of them had traded stocks—some for years. Buffett had just turned twenty. But he had matured beyond his years and was able to keep pace with his older classmates. Graham quickly realized that his youngest student had three important assets: talent, focus, and an eagerness to work hard.

In his classes Graham generally did not lecture. Instead he would pose a question or problem for his students to ponder. Buffett thrived in this environment. He almost always had well-reasoned answers to Graham's questions, with his photographic memory supplying facts from books, balance sheets, and annual reports to bolster his arguments. Sometimes an entire class period would evolve into a two-way conversation between Graham and Buffett. Soon, Graham began to invite his gifted student to social occasions at his home.

Graham frequently illustrated points being discussed in class with real examples from his brokerage firm, Graham-Newman Corporation. Whether he approved or not, these were construed as stock tips. His students, Buffett included, invested with Graham-Newman and sometimes bought the stocks their teacher talked about in class.

Buffett took a step that did not occur to his classmates. He researched Graham's business connections and discovered that Graham served on the board of directors of Government Employees Insurance Company (GEICO), a company based in Washington, D.C.

In the spring of 1951 Buffett traveled to Washington one Saturday to see his family. While there he took a side trip to the GEICO office. He pounded on the door until a janitor heard him. Buffett asked the janitor if anyone else happened to be working that day. The janitor allowed him to take the elevator to the sixth floor, where he found a top executive, Lorimer Davidson, hard at work.

Davidson had been the man who convinced Benjamin Graham to buy a controlling share of stock in GEICO. All afternoon Buffett questioned Davidson about the company. Davidson, initially shocked to hear such sophisticated queries coming from a twenty-year-old, volunteered answer after answer. Buffett learned that GEICO kept its costs low by selling through the mail rather than by employing insurance agents. He learned further that GEICO only sold automobile insurance policies to government workers—who, in addition to holding down steady jobs, statistically had safer driving records than the general public. As a result, GEICO was collecting far more money than it was paying out on accident claims.

Buffett's method of picking a profitable stock involved a careful study of annual reports and financial statements.
(Courtesy of Ninette Maumus/Alamy)

When Buffett returned to Manhattan, he sought the advice of other insurance company executives and stockbrokers. The insurance executives were skeptical about GEICO's small pool of policyholders and its sales-through-the-mail strategy. They said the stock was priced too high. Most stockbrokers had never even heard of the company. They too advised Buffett to avoid the risk.

Buffett did his own research on GEICO's financial records. By his reckoning, GEICO was exactly the kind of bargain enterprise that Graham talked about. Placing his faith in his teacher and his own diligent research, he invested in the company.

Upon graduating from Columbia in 1951—he received an A+ from Benjamin Graham—Buffett asked for a job at Graham-Newman. Graham not only turned him down, but also advised Buffett not to work in the stock market at all. Instead, he counseled Buffett to find an executive position in a growing industry.

Graham had two reasons for turning his star pupil away, but at the time he only told Buffett one of them: he feared another stock plunge. Graham thought the market had climbed about as high as it could before profit-seekers would begin to sell their stocks, thus driving prices down. In this view, Graham resembled many stockbrokers of his generation, who had suffered through the Great Depression.

Buffett did not learn Graham's second reason for refusing to hire him until several years later. Graham, who was Jewish, employed only fellow Jews at his brokerage. At the time, Wall Street brokerages practiced discrimination along racial and religious lines. Since many big firms would not hire Jews, Graham-Newman would not hire Gentiles.

Buffett could have stayed in Manhattan and worked for any of the large brokerage houses. But after spending time in the East, he understood better what it meant to live in Omaha. "I think it's a saner existence here," he recalled years later. "I used to feel, when I worked back in New York, that there were more stimuli just hitting me all the time, and if you've got the normal amount of adrenaline, you start responding to them. It may lead to crazy behavior after awhile. It's much easier to think here [in Omaha]."

Buffett returned home to Omaha and went to work with his father's firm, Buffett & Falk, as a stockbroker. But selling stocks in this manner proved unfulfilling for him. He had energy and ideas to spare. So he took a course in public speaking and accepted a position teaching the Graham method of investing in an adult-oriented night school, where some of his students were old enough to have been his parents.

Around the same time, Buffett met Susan Thompson, his sister's roommate at Northwestern University. Susie, as she was called, was beautiful and kind. Unlike Buffett's mother, who suffered from mood swings and sometimes launched tirades against her children, Susie was even-tempered and a good listener. She liked to help others solve their problems. Buffett fell in love with her instantly. Unfortunately, Susie had another boyfriend and paid little attention to her new, bespectacled suitor.

Aware that Susie did not share his affections, Buffett focused on winning over her father. He spent many hours in the home of William Thompson, a close friend and adviser to Howard Buffett. Thompson, like Warren Buffett, enjoyed cards, and the two men also shared a love of music. They played duets, Buffett strumming on the ukulele while Thompson worked the mandolin. Buffett made no effort to hide his feelings for Susie, and soon he had a valuable ally in his courtship.

At her father's urging, Susie began to date Warren Buffett. Over time she came to enjoy his company, delighting in his droll sense of humor and his enthusiasm for his work. After a few months, she accepted his marriage proposal.

Buffett was thrilled. He had not dated much during his school years, and Susie seemed perfect for him. They married in April 1952 and settled into a dingy three-room apartment in Omaha. Soon they welcomed their first child, a daughter they named for her mother. Baby Susie slept in an open dresser drawer.

Buffett promised his new wife that their humble circumstances were only temporary. He would soon become quite rich, and she would be able to buy anything she wanted. At first those promises of wealth seemed empty. As an investment counselor and stockbroker for his father's firm, Buffett found that customers doubted him because of his youth. He also invested in stocks no one had heard of before, like GEICO. Too many times, older men would consult Buffett, then buy their stocks with another broker. Hedging his own bets, Buffett bought a Texaco gas station in Omaha. He needed the profits from the business to help pay his bills.

As his new family scrimped and saved at home, Buffett invested more of his money in GEICO. Then he waited.

In just two years, the value of each share of GEICO doubled. The $8,000 Buffett had invested in 1952 became $16,000 in 1954. The few customers he had persuaded to follow his lead reaped similar gains. Naturally, they were inclined to return to him to invest their money. His commissions gradually began to grow.

Buffett and his wife, Susan *(Courtesy of Chris Kleponis/AFP/Getty Images)*

In those years Buffett worked out of his home. He spent most of the day reading annual reports and financial statements. With his unusually precise memory he could store and recall all sorts of information on every type of enterprise, from large national corporations to local department store chains. If Buffett found a company that fulfilled Ben Graham's criteria—and showed sound business principles—he added stock from the company to his investors' portfolios.

Unlike Graham, however, Buffett offered no stock tips—not in his classes, not to his investors, not even to his closest friends. He had begun to realize that he could achieve the most success by keeping silent about the best investment opportunities he discovered.

In 1954 one of Nebraska's two U.S. Senate seats became open with the death of Senator Hugh Butler. Howard Buffett, who two years earlier had retired from the House of Representatives, decided to compete for Butler's vacant seat. Warren Buffett threw his energies into campaigning on his father's behalf. Both men were deeply disappointed when Howard Buffett failed even to earn the support of Nebraska's Republican Party. At a state convention, moderate Republicans promoted another candidate, one who was not so critical of the popular president, Dwight D. Eisenhower. Howard Buffett, who once had to be convinced to run for office, suffered the indignity of rejection quietly, returning to his firm and to private life.

That same year, Warren Buffett received a telephone call from his favorite teacher. Ben Graham reported that integration had arrived on Wall Street. He invited Buffett to become an employee of Graham-Newman in New York.

Buffett had once begged to work at Graham-Newman simply for commissions. Now that he had an opportunity to enter the firm, he accepted without even asking how much his salary would be. He was paid $1,000 per month, which at that time was a fine upper-middle-class wage.

The Buffett family moved to White Plains, New York, a suburb of Manhattan. Soon after their arrival, they welcomed the birth of a son, Howard. Again the family lived frugally, even though Warren Buffett was earning a good salary. Every penny they saved on daily expenses, he insisted, could be invested in stocks. Once skeptical of her husband's bragging about his future wealth, Susie became a believer as, one after another, his well-researched investments reaped better-than-average returns.

During his employment at Graham-Newman, Buffett occasionally recommended a stock for which Ben Graham did not share his enthusiasm. Against his mentor's advice, Buffett sometimes put his own money on such a stock. But with his lightning-fast reading, the long hours he spent studying companies, and his boundless confidence, Buffett began to outperform Graham. The student had learned all that his teacher could impart. Buffett started to modify and improve upon Graham's strategies to suit a new generation and an era, the 1950s, when a strong economy began to be reflected in rising stock prices.

Graham and Buffett began to part ways on philosophical issues. Buffett liked to get to know companies from the inside, as he had the day he queried the GEICO executive. He also began investing in certain businesses because he was impressed by the people running them. Buffett—himself the product of four generations of hardworking and dedicated

Buffett touring Benjamin Moore Paints in 2001. Buffett usually investigates companies from the inside before deciding to invest in their stock. *(Courtesy of Gabe Palacio/Getty Images)*

businessmen—believed that a strong executive with imagination and enthusiasm could have a major impact on a company's profitability. When evaluating a potential investment, it simply made sense, in his view, to take into account not just the company but also the person who ran it. Passion for an enterprise could translate into profits.

Graham, by contrast, thought that his protégé placed too much emphasis on the personalities of executives. Graham's approach was strictly mathematical. When he was evaluating a company as a possible investment opportunity, it never would have occurred to him to find out how much passion the company's president had for the business.

On one point, however, Buffett and Graham agreed. While walking to lunch one day, Graham said to Buffett: "Money won't make any difference to you and me, Warren. We'll be the same. Our wives will just live better."

Graham's observation was dead on. Buffett did not dedicate himself to becoming wealthy so that he could enjoy an opulent lifestyle—he would, in fact, continue to live modestly even after he had become one of the world's richest people. Rather, he dedicated himself to becoming wealthy out of a sheer joy for earning money. Getting rich was a test of intellect, creativity, and perseverance, a puzzle to be assembled just for the thrill of the challenge. He began to gather the pieces.

FOUR

The Partnership

In 1956, Benjamin Graham folded the firm of Graham-Newman and moved to California. Warren Buffett faced another crossroads. He and his wife decided to move home to Omaha to be closer to their families.

Between 1950 and 1956 he had grown his fortune from $9,800 to $140,000. His personal portfolio had outperformed Graham-Newman's company portfolio by 17 percent. Buffett no longer needed to count his pennies; he had enough money to provide a comfortable life for himself and his family.

Back in Omaha, he rented a modest home for the family and allowed Susie to decorate it according to her tastes. Still, he urged her not to be too flamboyant. Money spent on home décor could not be invested.

Decades later, Buffett recalled that he experienced a short period of uncertainty upon his return to Omaha. "I didn't know what I was going to do," he said. "I had about $150,000 at that time, and I felt, you know, if I earned 10 percent it would be $15,000 a year and I could live big on that at the time." Buffett added that he had wanted to take more courses at a university, perhaps even study law.

Instead, through a combination of personal initiative and the prodding of his family and friends, he formed a financial partnership. On May 1, 1956, twenty-five-year-old Warren Buffett created Buffett Associates Ltd. Two of Buffett's seven partners—his aunt Alice and his sister Doris—were family members. The rest were longtime friends or acquaintances, including his former roommate from Wharton, Charles Peterson. Through these partners Buffett was able to raise $105,100. The $100 was his stake in the venture.

Buffett's quiet confidence and expert knowledge of stocks inspired trust in potential investors. By the end of 1957 he had persuaded several well-to-do doctors to join his partnership. This increased the capital Buffett could invest to nearly half a million dollars.

From the beginning, Buffett imposed strict rules on his partners. They could not ask how their money was being invested, and Buffett would not show them a portfolio. All of his transactions would be conducted in strictest secrecy. If partners did not like the rules, they could cash out—but only on December 31 of any year.

In exchange for that kind of faith, Buffett's partners were guaranteed a return of 4 percent each year, even if the investments lost money. Buffett pledged his personal funds for this coverage. If the investments earned more than 4 percent a year, Buffett would keep 25 percent of the difference and give his partners 75 percent.

In other words, an investment of $100,000 could be guaranteed to earn $4,000 the first year. But if the investment earned $20,000, Buffett would keep $4,000 (his share after the guaranteed return), and the partner would earn $16,000.

Buffett took no commissions for his work. The partnership was based solely on his ability to apply Graham's principles, as well as his own genius for absorbing and recalling information about companies.

In its first year, Buffett Associates Ltd. earned a 10 percent profit. Over the same period, the Dow Jones Industrial Average—a broad index of the stock market's performance—fell 8 percent.

In 1958, with this latest success under his belt, Buffett finally bought a house. It was a five-bedroom suburban stucco home on Farnam Street. The family had just settled in when the Buffetts' youngest son, Peter, was born.

Buffett jokingly called his house "Buffett's Folly," but he was secretly pleased with the price tag: $31,500. It seemed like a bargain for such a large home. He set up an office in a spare bedroom and spent long hours within its confines, analyzing companies and looking for bargain stocks.

Buffett continued to keep his decision-making secret for two reasons. First, he knew that if other stockbrokers in Omaha found out which stocks he was buying, they might rush to buy those stocks too. This would drive up the price per share, making it more costly for Buffett to acquire as much of the stock as he wanted. Second, Buffett invested with such brazen flair that some of his partners might have become skittish—and been inclined to cash out of the partnership—had they known how their money was being managed. Buffett thought nothing of sinking up to half of his funds

Buffett's house in Omaha, Nebraska *(Courtesy of AP Images/Nati Harnik)*

into a single company—and often that company seemed to be on the brink of disaster, its assets hidden and its stock price depressed.

One person with whom Buffett did discuss his investment ideas—and who would later become his most trusted adviser, his closest friend, and his business partner—was Charlie Munger. Six years Buffett's senior, Munger had grown up in Omaha and as a teen had even worked in the grocery store of Buffett's grandfather. But he and Warren Buffett did not meet until 1959, when they were introduced by a mutual

Buffett and Charlie Munger (left) speak to reporters at a news conference. *(Courtesy of AP Images/Nati Harnik)*

friend. Despite differences in the way they interact with other people—Buffett projected a good-natured, homespun charm, whereas Munger was intense and even brusque—the two men hit it off immediately.

Munger, a Harvard-trained attorney who had established a successful law practice in Los Angeles, desperately wanted a less hectic, more independent lifestyle. He had begun to invest, and he quickly recognized Buffett's genius in the field. For his part, Buffett was impressed by Munger's keen intellect and sharp judgment. Following their initial meeting, after Munger had returned to Los Angeles (he had been visiting family in Omaha), Buffett began to call him to ask for advice. Gradually the two men established an informal partnership, bouncing ideas off each other and investing in some of the same businesses. Both would become vastly wealthier as a result of their collaboration.

The late 1950s witnessed a bull market—a period during which stock values consistently rise—and Buffett Associates Ltd. doubled its money in just three years. More of his friends joined the partnership, including his old pinball partner from Washington, Donald Danly. But other potential investors, upon hearing about Buffett's secrecy, refused to give him their money.

After five years, during which the market in general was positive, Buffett's partnership had earned an astonishing 251 percent on its original investment. The Dow as a whole had risen 74 percent over the same period. Those who had placed their faith in the young man from Omaha had been richly rewarded.

In 1962 Buffett became a millionaire. His partnership—now called Buffett Partnership Ltd.—had $7.2 million in capital. From the modest number of original investors, the pool of partners now stood at ninety, and the minimum investment was $100,000.

The year 1962 was a watershed in the career of Warren Buffett for another reason. He began buying shares in a company that would become the flagship of his investment empire: Berkshire Hathaway. At the time, Berkshire was a group of New England textile mills, and its stock seemed like a bargain in the classic Ben Graham mold. Berkshire was trading at $7.60 per share, but the company was sitting on investments and assets that, if factored in, would make the stock worth more than $16 per share.

Secretly, Buffett bought up huge blocks of Berkshire Hathaway stock. Soon Buffett Partnership Ltd. owned more Berkshire stock than any other single investor. This gave the partnership a controlling interest in Berkshire and entitled it to a seat on the company's board of directors. Buffett initially concealed his investment by hiring someone to sit on the board in his place.

In 1963, however, he paid a visit to New Bedford, Massachusetts, the site of Berkshire Hathaway's corporate headquarters as well as its largest plant. After the visit, Buffett revealed his partnership's status as Berkshire's majority stockholder.

Buffett's decision to invest so heavily in a cluster of New England textile mills seemed questionable. For decades, the region's textile industry had been in decline, as mill owners increasingly moved their operations to the South. Fabric and clothing could be produced more cheaply there because of lower wages and because cotton is grown in the South, making transportation costs lower. The competitive position of New England's textile industry was further undermined by foreign-produced cloth, which was even cheaper than that manufactured in the southern states. By the 1960s, some industry analysts were predicting that New England's few remaining textile mills would be shuttered in the not-too-distant future.

Developments at Berkshire Hathaway lent support to that view. Shortly after Buffett Partnership gained a controlling interest in the company, Berkshire closed all but two of its plants and laid off 10,000 workers.

Buffett believed that the company suffered from incompetent management. He decided to wrest control of Berkshire from its longtime owner, Seabury Stanton, and Stanton's son and heir apparent, Jack. By 1965, having accumulated 49 percent of Berkshire's stock, Buffett could dictate what happened in the boardroom. He named himself director and, to run Berkshire's day-to-day operations, installed as company president an executive of his choosing.

Buffett promised the remaining 2,500 Berkshire Hathaway employees that he would keep the company's last two mills running. But he made no promises to modernize the plants or to develop new product lines—steps that would be necessary if Berkshire Hathaway hoped to remain viable in the long run as a textile manufacturer. Instead Buffett began to invest Berkshire Hathaway's cash reserves and yearly profits in other businesses.

One business that had drawn his interest was American Express, a financial services company. The years following World War II saw great prosperity in the United States, and more Americans traveled abroad than ever before. Many of these tourists were reluctant to carry large amounts of cash. Instead they bought, for a small service fee, American Express traveler's checks. Because they were paid for in advance and could be redeemed for local currency at any bank, the traveler's checks functioned like cash. But if they were lost or stolen, the checks could be voided, so the traveler would not lose money.

American Express also offered consumers another alternative to carrying large sums of cash. In 1958 the company introduced an early version of the now-ubiquitous credit card. It, like traveler's checks, proved extremely popular, and American Express thrived.

After acquiring Berkshire Hathaway, Buffett invested its cash reserves and yearly profits into promising companies like American Express. *(Courtesy of Edward Simons/Alamy)*

In November of 1963, however, trouble arose with a company owned by American Express. The subsidiary in question, a warehouse in New Jersey, had become part of a massive fraud. The warehouse had accepted tanker containers from a shady company called Allied Crude Vegetable Oil Refining. It issued Allied receipts for the containers, which Allied's owner then offered as collateral in obtaining $150 million in loans. When Allied went bankrupt, its creditors sought to sell the company's assets to repay these loans. Only then was it discovered that the tanker containers in the New Jersey warehouse contained not vegetable oil, but worthless seawater. Creditors demanded that the American

Express subsidiary—which had certified the contents of the tanker containers—take responsibility for repaying Allied's loans. The subsidiary did not have the financial resources to do this and itself faced bankruptcy.

By law, American Express was under no obligation to bail out its subsidiary; any financial exposure rested with the warehouse and its management. Nevertheless, the chief executive officer (CEO) of American Express vowed to make good on the debt. He believed that a company like his, which relied on public trust, must be above reproach. When news of this decision reached Wall Street, however, American Express stock plunged. Investors feared the $150 million payout might ruin the company.

From his office in Omaha, Warren Buffett followed these events closely. He also did some unconventional, down-home research. Buffett spent a few evenings eating at Gorat's, his favorite Omaha steak house. As he ate, he watched the other customers. Scandal or no, many of them continued to use their American Express cards to pay for their meals. Buffett also visited banks in Omaha. Tellers reported that customers were still buying American Express traveler's checks. People in Omaha evidently still had confidence in the American Express brand name. Buffett assumed that what held true in his hometown would also hold true in the rest of the country. He believed the long-term prospects for American Express remained good. Through his partnership, Buffett began to gobble up the company's stock.

Buffett's instincts proved correct. American Express settled with its subsidiary's creditors and weathered the scandal. Its stock rebounded, quickly rising to and then surpassing prescandal prices. Buffett, who had bought a huge share in the company while its stock prices were at a scandal-induced low, reaped a windfall.

In 1965, Buffett followed another hunch. While in New York on business, he saw the Walt Disney Productions' movie *Mary Poppins*. Buffett noticed the crowds of parents and children who waited in line to see the film, and he thought about the strength of the Disney brand name. He recognized, long before the advent of home video, that Disney's library of previously released children's movies—such as *Snow White and the Seven Dwarfs* and *Dumbo*—might also continue to generate profits.

Later Buffett took his children to Disneyland, using the occasion to get a closer look at how Disney ran its Anaheim, California, theme park. He liked what he saw.

Disneyland in 1955 *(Courtesy of AP Images)*

Buffett sank $4 million into Disney stock, acquiring 5 percent of the company for his partnership. It proved to be another shrewd investment. In 1967 Disney broke ground for another theme park, this one near Orlando, Florida. Over the years, Walt Disney World became an immensely popular vacation destination, and Buffett had a big stake in the profits the park generated.

As a result of Buffett's investments in companies like American Express and Disney, his partnership consistently outperformed the Dow Jones Industrial Average by significant margins. In 1965, for example, the Dow recorded a 14.2 percent rise, whereas Buffett's partnership gained 47.2 percent. The following year the Dow was down 15.6 percent, but Buffett's partnership rose 20.4 percent.

Buffett did his best to tamp down his partners' expectations. In spite of his excellent track record, he could not guarantee fantastic returns year after year. "Such results should be regarded as decidedly abnormal," he warned investors in his annual report for 1966.

Buffett had by this time outgrown his home office in the spare bedroom. So he rented office space in a modest highrise called Kiewit Plaza, which was located on Farnam Street just a few miles from his home. He hired a small staff, but they were given no information about his decisions. They handled incoming telephone calls and correspondence. Just as he had at home, Buffett spent most of his day in his small office, reading or talking to Charlie Munger on the telephone. He decorated the space with a portrait of his father, who died in the spring of 1964.

FIVE

A New Direction

By 1967, when he turned thirty-seven, Warren Buffett's net worth stood at $10 million. He had fulfilled his childhood resolution to be rich.

Yet Buffett did not surround himself with the trappings of wealth. He and his family lived modestly. Unlike other members of the ultra-rich class, they never bought a villa in Europe, never threw lavish parties, never sought to hobnob with movie stars or socialites. Warren and Susie Buffett sent their children not to an exclusive private academy but to the same public school Warren had attended. The children were encouraged to earn their own pocket money and were given allowances equal to those of their friends.

Warren Buffett's pleasures were simple. He enjoyed playing bridge, hosting friends for dinner parties, and music.

Most of all, however, he loved the challenge of investing. Though he had already made a fortune, Buffett remained completely immersed in his work. He spent most of his time cloistered in his office, reading financial reports, studying balance sheets, telephoning Charlie Munger—all in his never-ending pursuit of solid investments.

With his single-minded focus on business, Buffett relied heavily on his wife to keep his household—and his life—running smoothly. Susie assumed primary responsibility for raising the couple's children. She also bought her husband clothes, and picked out a Cadillac for him after he complained that the family Volkswagen was too small to accommodate visiting clients.

By October of 1967, the Buffett Partnership was worth $65 million—a staggering sum, considering that the fund had started with about $100,000 and had existed for little more than a decade.

By the late 1960s, Buffett had been managing his investment partnership for about a dozen years. During that time, the value of a share in the partnership had increased thirty-fold. Buffett had made his partners—and himself—fantastic amounts of money.

Many of Buffett's partners anticipated more years of extraordinary returns. More money than ever was being pumped into the stock market, thereby driving up share prices. Wall Street was in the midst of a bull market, and Buffett's investors saw no reason they should not continue to benefit from the good times.

The emergence of a new generation of stockbroker added to this optimism. Young and energetic, these stockbrokers garnered considerable attention from the media. They insisted that everyone, not just Americans with high incomes, could invest in and make money from the stock market. These maverick brokers were not especially interested in a company's underlying strength or its long-term prospects. Rather, they monitored stock prices hour by hour or even minute by minute. And they bought and sold frequently, taking advantage of fluctuations in prices to make a profit.

Warren Buffett had a different philosophy of investing: he was interested in the long term. He sought solid companies that had good prospects for profitability but whose stocks were currently undervalued. In the bull market of the late 1960s, however, Buffett had trouble finding the bargain stocks he favored. He believed that the market was actually overvalued.

Buffett had made his money by running counter to prevailing opinion. When everyone started to buy, he sold. He had invested $13 million in American Express at the company's darkest hour. In 1967 he sold the stock for $33 million. He also sold his Disney stock at a 50 percent profit.

Other ventures did not prove so profitable. He had bought a department store chain based in Baltimore and another in the South. Neither one showed much growth. The Berkshire Hathaway mills continued to eke out a profit each year, but Buffett had invested that company's assets in other places.

The bull market carried his marginal businesses along, but Buffett felt that the bubble might burst at any moment. His partners had become accustomed to fantastic returns. Now he believed he could no longer play his game. Everything was overpriced.

Buffett could see only one solution to his problem. On May 29, 1969, he stunned his investors by informing them that he was ending the partnership. "I am not attuned to this market environment," he said, "and I don't want to spoil a decent record by trying to play a game I don't understand just so I can go out a hero."

Buffett sold off all but two assets in the partnership's portfolio: the southern department store chain and Berkshire Hathaway. Buffett told his partners that he planned to keep his stock in these two companies, hoping that he might earn a modest 10 percent annually on them. He told his partners that they too could buy Berkshire Hathaway stock and ride with him if they liked. The price stood at $43 per share. Buffett had bought control of the company for $7.50 per share.

Some of Buffett's partners ended their association with him. These investors believed that Buffett had lost his touch, and they thought his textile mill enterprise was likely to fail. Yet many more partners invested in Berkshire Hathaway stock. Their faith in Buffett could not be shaken.

The Buffett Partnership had proven stressful for its creator because his investors had come to expect huge returns. Freed from those expectations, Buffett still longed to make more money. He chose to do so in innovative ways.

One of his first decisions was to call his entire enterprise "Berkshire Hathaway," even though he had diversified the company's holdings. Buffett liked tradition, and the name sounded solid and old-fashioned. Plus, it fit his longtime preference for conducting his affairs in relative secrecy. Although Berkshire Hathaway was a publicly traded company, casual traders might assume the company was merely a textile-manufacturing concern.

If Buffett had previously made most of his money by investing in stocks, he now turned to a different strategy: buying companies outright. To pursue that strategy, Buffett needed vast amounts of cash on hand. Through his purchase of an insurance company, National Indemnity of Omaha, Buffett had figured out a way to generate the necessary cash.

The insurance business is deceptively simple. The customer regularly pays a sum of money, called a premium, to keep a policy with the insurance company in force. The policy obligates the insurance company to cover the customer's financial losses if a specified event occurs (for example, if the customer has a car accident or suffers a house fire). But insurance companies do not simply hold on to premiums until they have to pay out claims. Rather, they invest a large portion of the pool of premiums from all their customers. This earns the insurance companies a profit.

At the time Buffett bought National Indemnity, most insurance companies invested their collected premiums—called the "float"—in low-risk (and hence low-return) investments. Buffett was more daring. Essentially betting that he would not have to pay out many large claims at the same time, he used the float to buy other cash-generating entities, including entire companies. In this manner he was able to reap much higher profits than other insurance companies.

Buffett soon found another company that generated even more floating revenue than National Indemnity. He teamed with Charlie Munger to begin buying control of Blue Chip Stamps in 1970. Supermarkets and other stores bought stamps issued by the company. The stamps, which the stores gave out to loyal customers, could be redeemed for household items like toasters or pots and pans. Often, however, people lost the stamps, forgot to redeem them, or simply did not collect enough to buy anything. Nevertheless, the stores paid up front for the stamps, so plenty of money rolled in to Blue

Chip's coffers. Buffett and Munger used that money as ready cash for investment.

The business relationship between the two became even closer. In 1971 Buffett bought a vacation property in Laguna Beach, California. While his family relaxed on the beach, however, Buffett spent long days consulting with Munger, who owned a home nearby. Buffett also bounced investment ideas off his old mentor, Ben Graham. Together they plotted ways to squeeze profits out of underperforming businesses—sometimes by laying off workers and closing plants, but most often by using the idle financial assets of companies to buy other enterprises.

Buffett always made a rule of buying stocks or entire companies that he as a consumer could understand. One of these came into his possession in 1972, after Munger telephoned his friend and urged him to buy a company called See's Candies Shops. Buffett, who had never heard of See's Candies, initially demurred. But after doing a little research of his own, he changed his mind. Buffett discovered that See's dominated the chocolate market in California, where the company had a recognizable name and, it seemed, a stable base of customers. See's chocolates cost more than other brands, but its loyal customers were willing to pay more. Buffett called Munger back and instructed him to make an offer of $25 million for the franchise through Blue Chip Stamps.

This was the largest sum Buffett had ever paid for a business. He knew next to nothing about how chocolate was made. But he knew that people loved to eat it—and he understood the importance of a recognizable brand name.

Buffett's purchase of See's Candies also reflected his commitment to long-term ownership. He would not realize

Buffett (far right) and Charlie Munger stand with a See's Candies model and See's Candies president Charles Huggins (left). *(Courtesy of Wirepix/Tannen Maury/The Image Works)*

much profit if he held the company for a few years and then resold it. Instead he has kept See's Candies among Berkshire Hathaway's holdings since 1972.

At the beginning of the 1970s, the stock market took a downturn. Armed with his insurance float money, Buffett again began to search for bargain stocks. After some characteristically diligent research, Buffett concluded that newspaper publishing could be a reliably profitable business.

Buffett actually borrowed money to buy large blocks of stock in The Washington Post Company, owner of one of the country's best-known daily newspapers, the *Washington Post*. The company also owned *Newsweek* magazine as well as several television stations.

The CEO of The Washington Post Company, Katharine Graham—who also served as the *Post*'s publisher—initially worried that Buffett was planning to wrest control of the newspaper from her. After the two met, however, her mind was put at ease.

Buffett and Graham hit it off immediately, and their friendship would bring tangible benefits to both. Buffett, a member of The Washington Post Company's board of directors by virtue of his large stockholdings, shared his financial and business acumen with Graham. She, in turn, introduced Buffett to the world of national politics and high society. Buffett—a man who had spent his career working behind the scenes in Omaha—discovered that he enjoyed the newfound attention. Despite his higher profile, however, Buffett remained unassuming. Even at the most lavish dinner party he would request a soft drink. Once, when offered a glass of wine from an expensive vintage, Buffett covered his glass and joked, "I'll take the cash."

Katharine Graham *(Courtesy of AP Images)*

His friendship with Katharine Graham aside, Buffett's purchase of Washington Post stock turned out to be another excellent investment. Investigative reporters at the *Post* played a leading role in exposing a wide-reaching scandal known as Watergate, which began with a botched burglary of the Democratic National Convention's headquarters in June 1972. The unfolding story riveted the attention of the country as it became apparent that officials in the administration of President Richard M. Nixon were involved. By the time the scandal forced Nixon to resign in August 1974, the *Post*'s circulation had increased greatly as a result of its coverage.

Buffett spotted another excellent opportunity in 1976. GEICO was facing bankruptcy. In 1975 the insurance company reported a loss of $126 million, triggering a massive sell-off of its stock. (Buffett had sold his own GEICO shares, at a considerable profit, before the company's troubles.) From a 1974 high of $42 per share, GEICO stock had plunged to a pitiful $2 per share.

The company's crisis developed because GEICO had begun to insure more high-risk drivers, while the cost of claims rose and individual states tried to curb rate increases. In an attempt to stem the red ink, GEICO's new president, John J. Byrne Jr., laid off thousands of employees, quit doing business in certain states, and cancelled policies elsewhere. Most observers concluded, however, that the business was doomed.

Buffett knew that his former teacher, Ben Graham, still held a significant stake in GEICO. Moreover, he continued to believe that the way GEICO did business—by selling policies directly to consumers, without insurance agents—was sound. He decided to take the measure of Byrne to determine whether to invest in the company.

If Byrne had failed to earn Buffett's esteem, GEICO would have closed its doors. But Byrne impressed Buffett as an aggressive and determined chief executive. Buffett invested $4 million in GEICO's devalued stock and persuaded an investment firm, Salomon Brothers, to raise capital for the company by underwriting an additional $75 million in stock. These funds allowed GEICO to begin paying its bills and attracting customers again.

One of the biggest buyers of Salomon's GEICO stock offering turned out to be Warren Buffett's Berkshire Hathaway. Berkshire's stake in the company quickly rose from $4 million to $23 million, making it GEICO's principal shareholder. Buffett gave the company time to rebuild its competitive edge. And when GEICO recovered, Buffett was wealthier than ever.

Six

Showdown in Buffalo

Having invested in The Washington Post Company as well as in Knight Ridder, a company that owned a chain of newspapers, Buffett considered buying a paper outright. He had several criteria. First, the paper had to be in a big city, or at least serve a big market of city and suburbs combined. Second, it had to lead its competitors in circulation and advertising revenue. Third, it had to be a brand name with customer loyalty. He found just such a newspaper in the *Buffalo Evening News*.

Buffalo is a large, diverse city at the eastern edge of Lake Erie in New York State. In the late 1970s it had a significant working-class population. Many workers preferred to get their newspaper in the evenings at the end of a shift. They subscribed to the *Evening News*. The rival newspaper, the *Buffalo Courier-Express,* published in the mornings.

Only half as many people read the *Courier-Express* as the *Evening News.*

The *Evening News* had been a family-owned business with a unionized labor force and state-of-the-art printing facilities. With the death of its chairwoman, the family decided to sell.

Buffett tried to persuade Katharine Graham to purchase the *Evening News* through The Washington Post Company, but she was deterred by the newspaper's strong unions. Graham saw another negative: The *Evening News* did not publish a Sunday edition. That slot had been filled by the *Courier-Express,* and the Sunday circulation and advertising had helped the *Courier-Express* overcome its second-class status during the week. The only way to dominate the newspaper market in Buffalo would be to create a Sunday newspaper for the *Evening News.*

Buffett thought it could be done. He bought the *Buffalo Evening News* early in 1977 for $32.5 million, again using funds from Blue Chip Stamps. By the spring of that year he began dropping hints to the paper's management that he wanted to expand to a seven-day schedule. He flew back and forth between Omaha and Buffalo, helping the staff of his newest enterprise design and prepare to produce a Sunday edition. By November, the *Evening News* Sunday paper was set to launch.

Residents of Buffalo—as well as advertisers—recognized that the city could not support the *Courier-Express* and the *Evening News* if both ran on Sunday. Some merchants promised not to buy ads in the Sunday *Evening News.*

Then, just weeks before the Sunday launch date, lawyers for the *Courier-Express* filed suit against the *Evening News.*

A *Buffalo News* box. Buffett purchased the *Buffalo News* in 1977. (*Courtesy of Harry Scull Jr./Getty Images*)

The lawyers had learned that Buffett's paper planned to give its Sunday edition away for free during a five-week promotional period. The only possible explanation, they asserted, was that the *Evening News* sought to encourage readers of the rival Sunday paper to switch. And, *Courier-Express* lawyers claimed, the Sunday edition of the *Evening News* would ultimately put the *Courier-Express* out of business. This would leave Buffalo with only one newspaper; they argued that such a monopoly would violate the 1890 federal law known as the Sherman Antitrust Act.

The *Courier-Express* fought Buffett in the court of public opinion. The paper ran editorials and long articles about its lawsuit. Its writers pointed out that Buffett had no ties to Buffalo, whereas the *Courier-Express* had been owned by a Buffalo family for decades.

When the *Courier-Express* lawsuit was heard in federal court, Buffett took the stand in defense of his decision to create a Sunday edition. He denied any intention of running the *Courier-Express* out of business. His decision to buy the *Evening News*, he said, was based completely on its profitability as a company, and he was within his rights to enhance the company's profitability even further. He also stated that he believed the *Courier-Express* brand would survive its Sunday competition, since people stick to their reading habits.

The trial judge sided with the *Courier-Express*. While the judge did not deny the *Evening News* the right to publish on Sunday, he issued a ruling that contained restrictions that would hamper circulation, solicitation of advertising, and promotion to potential readers. For example, the ruling put an end to the *Evening News*'s plans to offer seven days of newspapers for the price of six. Subscribers would have to buy the paper at face value.

Worse, the negative publicity eroded support for the *Evening News*. Working-class Buffalo readers expressed solidarity with employees of the *Courier-Express*, who stood to lose their jobs if their paper's hold on Sunday readership slipped. Not surprisingly, the Sunday edition of the *Evening News* sold very poorly, and the newspaper began to lose money even on its weekly subscriptions.

Buffett had invested a great deal of money in the *Evening News*. True to his philosophy of patience and long-term investment, he hired a manager he respected, and he encouraged the staff of the *Evening News* to pursue the highest quality in their journalism. The rivalry between the two newspapers raged. Both lost money. Then, in 1979, an appeals court reversed the decision against the *Evening News*. The judges on the U.S. Court of Appeals believed Buffett's statement that he did not buy the newspaper to run his competitor out of business. The *Evening News* was suddenly free to do as it pleased with its Sunday edition.

The damage had been done, however. In circulation the Sunday *Evening News* lagged far behind its competitor. At the same time, both newspapers lost daily circulation and advertising because of difficult economic conditions in Buffalo. Buffett had bought a profitable paper, but now it was losing millions of dollars each year. For the first time in his career, Warren Buffett looked vulnerable.

When a powerful union, the International Brotherhood of Teamsters, called a strike against the *Evening News* in 1980, the newspaper's end appeared imminent. Buffett told his management negotiators to let all the workers know that a strike would ruin the business, and he meant it. Ultimately the Teamsters accepted a compromise. The paper limped on.

The *Evening News* got a boost after the *Courier-Express* was bought by a larger chain of papers headquartered in Minneapolis, Minnesota. No longer could the *Courier-Express* claim that it was locally owned. Gradually, Buffett saw circulation of his Sunday edition climb, and in 1982 the *Courier-Express* finally folded. That same year, the *Evening News* changed its name to the *Buffalo News* and began publishing a morning edition.

Having won a battle it appeared he would lose, Buffett reveled in the newspaper's renewed profitability. In an annual

Buffett in 1980 *(Courtesy of Lee Balterman/Time Life Pictures/Getty Images)*

letter to Berkshire Hathaway shareholders, he wrote: "Although our profit margins in 1983 were about average for newspapers such as the *News*, the paper's performance, nevertheless, was a significant achievement considering the economic and retailing environment in Buffalo."

Buffett turned fifty on August 30, 1980. With his wife at his side, he marked the occasion with a black-tie gala at the Metropolitan Club in New York City. The ritzy affair demonstrated the ease with which Buffett could now move in high society. Yet it did not mean that he had finally embraced the ostentatious ways of the ultra rich. Although *Forbes* magazine ranked Buffett high on its list of the world's wealthiest individuals, he continued to live modestly in Omaha. In little more than a decade Buffett had increased the value of Berkshire Hathaway stock from $43 to $375 per share, yet he paid himself an annual salary of just $50,000 to manage the company.

But not all was right in Buffett's world. In 1977 his wife Susie—often described as a free spirit—moved out of their Omaha home and rented an apartment in San Francisco. According to friends, Susie's move was not motivated by dissatisfaction with her husband but by her desire to pursue a career as a nightclub singer. She never filed for divorce.

Nevertheless, Buffett was devastated by his wife's departure. "Susie was the sun and the rain in my garden for twenty-five years," he confessed to his sister Doris.

Although Buffett focused on his work, as he had always done, he was extremely lonely. It was Susie Buffett who proposed a solution. While singing in an Omaha nightclub, Susie had met and befriended a Latvian-born cocktail waitress named Astrid Menks. On a visit to Omaha, Susie introduced

Buffet walking with Astrid Menks in 2006 *(Courtesy of AP Images/Elaine Thompson)*

the thirty-one-year-old Menks to her husband and encouraged them to spend time together. By 1978 Menks had moved into the Buffett home on Farnam Street.

The arrangement evidently suited everyone. Susie Buffett and Menks remained friends. Warren Buffett spent vacations with his wife, who also accompanied him on important business trips and at formal events. When Buffett was at home in Omaha, Menks was his daily companion. The Buffetts and Menks even sent out Christmas cards signed by all three of them.

"I really like my life," Buffett remarked in the late 1970s. "I've *arranged* my life so that I can do what I want."

With his home life satisfied, what he wanted, above all, was to grow Berkshire Hathaway.

SEVEN

The Oracle of Omaha

By the early 1980s stock analysts and savvy investors recognized that Berkshire Hathaway was much more than a textile manufacturer. It was a holding company—a company that has a controlling interest in, or owns totally, other firms.

Berkshire had interests in a diverse array of businesses, from newspaper publishing to candy making to auto insurance. What unified this odd array of holdings was simply Warren Buffett's belief that the companies in question could produce consistent profits over the long haul.

Buffett's ability to pick winning companies that other investors overlooked earned him the nickname the Oracle of Omaha. His reputation on Wall Street became such that news that Berkshire was investing in a company could cause the company's stock price to rise as much as 10 percent in a single day. Wall Street insiders watched his every move closely. Amateur investors learned about Buffett from short analytical pieces he began to contribute to the nation's financial periodicals. Some investors even bought a few shares of Berkshire Hathaway simply because that entitled them to receive the company's annual report, prepared by Buffett.

Berkshire Hathaway's annual reports were unusual. They contained none of the bright graphics or glossy photos found in the reports other large companies sent to their shareholders. Rather, Buffet's reports consisted of simply formatted text interspersed with tables of numbers. Yet Buffett, Berkshire's chairman—who himself read thousands of annual reports every year—still managed to make his annual report interesting. In addition to the requisite financial statements, information about business activities, and details on stock performance, Buffett's reports contained generous helpings of his homespun humor. They also documented the business philosophy of Buffett and Charlie Munger—who became Berkshire Hathaway's vice chairman after Blue Chip Stamps was folded into Berkshire in 1983—and detailed the way this philosophy applied to Berkshire Hathaway.

One pillar of Buffett's business philosophy is that great companies begin with managers who are genuinely enthusiastic about their business rather than simply interested in making a lot of money. Buffett considered this especially important, often retaining the chief executives of the companies Berkshire Hathaway buys, believing they know much better than he about how to run their business. "What I must understand," Buffett noted, "is why someone will continue to get out of bed in the morning once they have all the money they could want. Do they love the business, or do they love the money?"

In 1983 the Oracle of Omaha bought a 90 percent share in a company whose owner clearly passed Buffett's test for passion. Eighty-nine-year-old Rose Blumkin, who had emigrated from Russia in 1917, had been selling furniture in Omaha for fifty-five years. Though she had never attended school, Mrs. B—as Blumkin was affectionately known—had built her Nebraska Furniture Mart from a small basement storeroom into the most successful retailer of furniture and carpet in the state. She combined business savvy with an incredible work ethic. Mrs. B managed to buy her merchandise at very low costs and worked every day of every week. In her later years, after bringing her sons and grandsons into the business, Mrs. B made the carpet department her domain. She was always on hand to personally assist a customer—even after she had to resort to riding in a wheelchair to get around.

Rose Blumkin *(Courtesy of AP Images)*

Buffett had followed her career for decades and admired her as much as some of the world-famous CEOs in his sphere of influence. "I'd rather wrestle grizzlies than compete with Mrs. B and her progeny," Buffett wrote in his annual letter to shareholders in 1983. "They buy brilliantly, they operate at expense ratios competitors don't even dream about, and they then pass on to their customers much of the savings. It's the ideal business—one built upon exceptional value to the customer that in turn translates into exceptional economics for its owners."

The $60 million Buffett paid for the Nebraska Furniture Mart constituted Berkshire Hathaway's single largest purchase to date. Buffett thought he was getting a good deal, however. He believed that he was buying more than just a growing furniture store. He was also buying a motivated force of managers in the person of Mrs. B and her sons and grandsons.

The purchase allowed Mrs. B to allot money to members of her family who wanted to pursue other interests. She never would have sold, however, had Buffett not allowed her to stay on as the head of the enterprise. He enjoyed taking top executives of major corporations to the store to show them how well run and profitable it was.

In 1985, while the Nebraska Furniture Mart continued to flourish, the last remaining Berkshire Hathaway mill, in New Bedford, Massachusetts, finally closed its doors. Buffett did not sell the mill to another textile producer. He could not find any buyers. Instead he liquidated, thrusting four hundred skilled workers out of their jobs. The workers sought extra severance pay. Buffett gave them one additional month of pay, as well as opportunities for job retraining. Still, most of the workers could not find employment that paid as well as their jobs in the mill.

The mill workers resented Buffett's decision to close. They had sacrificed raises and benefits to hold on to their jobs. In the end, however, they faced the reality of American economics in the 1980s. Domestic manufacturers could not compete with foreign textile producers, which paid their employees a fraction of what American workers earned. Berkshire Hathaway was not alone in this dilemma—more than 250 American textile mills closed between 1980 and 1985.

In his 1985 annual letter to his stockholders, Buffett expressed little regret about his decision to close the mill. He did praise the workers throughout the entire operation for their cooperation, but he stated that he should have closed the mill a decade sooner. Had he done so, he would have deprived the mill staff of ten years' worth of salaries and benefits.

Buffett also defended his decision to invest the mill's funds in other enterprises—especially insurance—rather than plowing the profits into machinery upgrades and higher salaries within the textile business. "I . . . feel it inappropriate for even an exceptionally profitable company to fund an operation once it appears to have unending losses in prospect," he wrote. Buffett reinforced this point with a colorful analogy. "Should you find yourself in a chronically-leaking boat," he noted, "energy devoted to changing vessels is likely to be more productive than energy devoted to patching leaks."

Ironically, the mill closed after a year in which Berkshire Hathaway stock leaped 23 percent in value. Buffett had devoted his energy to changing vessels. Had he not, the end of the mill might have marked the end of his career.

Instead, he faced the enviable problem of managing an already huge, and still growing, pool of capital. Buffett believed that 1985 offered scant opportunities to buy bargain stocks. The nation had emerged from a recession, and stocks were either trading at market value or above. In that climate he turned elsewhere to invest.

Buffett received a call from an old friend, Tom Murphy, the CEO of a broadcasting and publishing empire called Capital Cities. The company owned local television stations all over the country as well as a variety of magazines and newspapers.

Murphy had recently learned that the American Broadcasting Company (ABC) was going to be sold or possibly dismantled in a hostile takeover. Buffett owned some ABC stock through Berkshire Hathaway. Murphy came to him for advice. He wanted to know whether Buffett thought Capital Cities ought to make a bid to buy ABC. The merger would make Capital Cities the largest broadcasting entity in the United States. But, by

Tom Murphy *(Courtesy of Mat Szwajkos/Getty Images)*

leaving Capital Cities short on cash, it might put Murphy's company at risk of a hostile takeover—unless one extremely wealthy investor financed the merger. Murphy politely asked if Berkshire Hathaway could be that investor.

The deal posed two problems. Under rules of the Federal Communications Commission (FCC), one owner could not have two news-producing outlets in the same market. Berkshire Hathaway owned a newspaper, the *Buffalo News,* in a city where Capital Cities owned a television station. After all his struggles to make the newspaper profitable, Buffett did not want to sell it. Murphy agreed to sell the television station instead. Yet another problem loomed. By law Buffett could not serve on the board of directors of The Washington Post Company—a position he loved—and on the board of directors of Capital Cities/ABC. Buffett decided to resign from the board of the Post.

Through Berkshire Hathaway he offered to buy 3 million shares of stock at the market price of $172.50 per share. The deal, worth slightly more than $500 million, would allow Capital Cities to buy ABC outright and keep it together—a prospect that pleased ABC's founder, Leonard Goldenson.

Buffett and Murphy brokered a deal that would have stunned Buffett's old mentor Ben Graham. The final price per share for the Capital Cities purchase of ABC stood at sixteen times *more* than earnings. ABC's lawyers had also insisted that shareholders of ABC be able to use specially issued warrants to buy Capital Cities stock. This acquisition was hardly a bargain for Berkshire Hathaway.

Buffett reassured his stockholders, reiterating his philosophy of investing for the long term. "We should note that we expect to keep permanently our three primary holdings, Capital

Cities/ABC, Inc., GEICO Corporation, and The Washington Post," he wrote. "Even if these securities were to appear significantly overpriced, we would not anticipate selling them, just as we would not sell See's or Buffalo Evening News if someone were to offer us a price far above what we believe those businesses are worth."

During the fall of 1985, Buffett read that the Scott Fetzer Company—a firm he had long been watching—also faced a hostile takeover. Through one of its divisions, Scott Fetzer published the *World Book Encyclopedia*, which for generations had reigned as the most popular American reference book. Libraries bought new editions every few years, and door-to-door salespeople peddled the books to parents of schoolchildren. Buffett remembered reading *World Book Encyclopedia* as a child.

Buffett wrote to Scott Fetzer's chairman, Ralph Schey, and offered to protect Schey's company from the stock speculators who were attempting to engineer the hostile takeover. In return for selling Scott Fetzer to Berkshire Hathaway, Schey would receive a guarantee that his company would not be dismantled and that he would retain his job. Just months after plowing some $500 million into Capital Cities/ABC, Buffett spent $315 million for Scott Fetzer. Yet another American icon, *World Book Encyclopedia,* became nestled under the Berkshire Hathaway umbrella.

In October of 1985, *Forbes* magazine named Buffett to its list of American billionaires. With his name enshrined among America's very wealthiest, Buffett emerged from the world of finance into a more general fame. Newspapers and magazines began to court him for feature stories, asking him about his private life. He declined to discuss such matters

Buffett posing for a photo in 1989 *(Courtesy of Rob Kinmonth/Time Life Pictures/Getty Images)*

in the press. Rather, the Oracle of Omaha talked and wrote about what he knew best: a sound philosophy of investing, learned from Benjamin Graham at Columbia University and refined by a lifetime of observing how great businesses were built and run.

Old-fashioned as Berkshire's portfolio might have seemed, it continued to post double-digit gains every year, no matter how the general stock market performed. Three times during the 1980s—in 1982, 1985, and 1989—the gain in per-share value of Berkshire stock topped 40 percent. In 1985, the year he bought Capital Cities/ABC stock and Scott Fetzer, Buffett saw his company's stock gain 48.2 percent in value. He consistently outperformed the Standard & Poor 500 stock averages (a measuring tool similar to the Dow Jones), once by more than 36 percentage points.

Throughout this amazing run, Buffett constantly warned his investors that this kind of success could not continue. As his pool of financial resources grew, he said, he would find it harder and harder to make deals that would result in annual gains of more than 20 percent.

Buffett never ducked the challenge, however. Working with Munger and his growing pool of topnotch company managers, he continued to search for ways to grow Berkshire Hathaway's stock.

Eight

For the Love of Cherry Coke

Warren Buffett has always joked about his fondness for colas. Whether attending a black-tie affair or a business luncheon, he has always opted for soft drinks rather than alcohol. For many years Pepsi was his beverage of choice. In the early 1960s he began to lace his Pepsi with cherry-flavored syrup. Then he found a product that eliminated his need to mix and stir.

In 1985 the Coca-Cola Company introduced a new product, Cherry Coke. Alerted ahead of time by a Coca-Cola executive, Buffett eagerly tried the beverage. He loved it.

Buffett had been watching the Coca-Cola Company for many years. He used his standard method to chart Coke's progress: the annual report. Coke displayed one of Buffett's favorite traits. It was a well-known brand name, not only in the United States but all over the world. The flagship beverage celebrated its hundredth anniversary in 1986. Earlier in

The Coca-Cola Company introduced Cherry Coke in 1985. *(Courtesy of Al Freni/Time & Life Pictures/Getty Images)*

the decade, its customer loyalty had been proven when the Coca-Cola Company announced that it had created a "New Coke" that was supposedly better tasting than the traditional formula. Americans stocked up on the old variety and begged the company to return to its original formula. The company listened and brought back its former flavoring. Meanwhile, Coca-Cola's other brands—Dr. Pepper, Diet Coke, and Sprite among them—enjoyed brisk sales.

Still, in the bull market of the 1980s, Buffett felt that the company's stock was trading too high. Worse, in Buffett's opinion, Coca-Cola had invested in companies that had nothing to do with soft drinks. These included Columbia Pictures, a movie studio. Buffett thought that Coke should stick to its core products and try to build their market share. He also questioned the company's lack of aggressiveness in foreign markets. He thought Coke could be performing better in densely populated countries like China and India.

In 1987 the stock market fell sharply in what traders call a correction. Even Buffett's Berkshire Hathaway took a hit, dropping more than $1,000 per share. Although he lost $342 million that year, Buffett was insulated from worse consequences by his ownership of whole companies like GEICO and the Nebraska Furniture Mart, now the largest furniture store in the nation. While other traders viewed the downturn with horror, Buffett saw opportunities. Bear markets offered chances to buy bargain stocks.

Anonymously, Buffett began buying huge chunks of Coca-Cola stock. Coke had lost a quarter of its value in the crash, but Buffett thought highly of its top managers, CEO Roberto C. Goizueta and president Donald R. Keough. Goizueta and Keough began to buy back Coke stock and divest themselves

In 1987, Buffett started buying large amounts of Coca-Cola stock.
(Courtesy of AP Images/Douglas C. Pizac)

of the unrelated business ventures. They decided to put more emphasis on the sale of Coke abroad. They became concerned about a hostile takeover when they noticed that some entity had purchased more than $1 billion in the company and seemed eager to buy even more.

Keough noticed that the buyer's orders were coming from the Midwest. He correctly deduced that Berkshire Hathaway was Coke's new suitor. When he phoned Buffett to ask why Berkshire Hathaway was buying so much stock, Buffett joked that he simply liked Cherry Coke. Buffett asked Keough not to tell anyone that Berkshire was behind the surge in buying. If the information had become public, the stock would have soared.

As much as he liked Cherry Coke, Buffett did not invest in the Coca-Cola brand because he drank it. "There just comes a point there's a tipping point . . . in terms of knowledge you've accumulated over a period of time," Buffett said in 2006. "Roberto and Don were doing a terrific job. Nothing bad was going to happen to Coca-Cola, so I started buying it. . . . We put overall about $1 billion into it and it's probably worth about $8 billion now."

Around the time of his billion-dollar purchase of Coke stock, Buffett became involved in another large deal. This one would ultimately embroil the quiet investor from Omaha in a national controversy.

John Gutfreund, chairman of the Wall Street investment firm Salomon Brothers, appealed to Buffett for help in 1987. The two had been friends for more than a decade. Salomon Brothers had earned a reputation for aggressive investing with solid returns. In the bear market of the late 1980s, however, the company began to sag. Its major shareholder wanted to sell, and the buyer with the most interest was a corporate raider named Ronald O. Perelman. Perelman had a reputation for buying companies and firing their CEOs.

Gutfreund hoped Buffett would be willing to stifle Perelman's takeover attempt. Buffett flew to New York,

John Gutfreund *(Courtesy of AP Images/David Cantor)*

where he and Gutfreund negotiated a deal. Berkshire Hathaway invested $700 million in Salomon Brothers convertible preferred stock. Unlike common stock, convertible preferred carries no voting rights but includes a guaranteed dividend; it also must be held for a specified period, after which it can be sold or converted into common stock at the shareholder's discretion. Through this deal, Buffett got a guaranteed 15 percent return for Berkshire Hathaway, and he demanded and received two seats on Salomon's board of directors—one for himself, and one for Charlie Munger. The deal was a winning proposition for Gutfreund as well. He was able to stave off a hostile takeover by Perelman—and thereby to save his job and the jobs of his staff members.

Two years later, Buffett used a similar arrangement to acquire a controlling interest in Gillette, a company that dominated the American razor market. Berkshire's $600 million purchase of Gillette convertible preferred stock enabled the company, like Salomon Brothers, to avoid a hostile takeover planned by Perelman. Gillette was the kind of company Buffett favored: it enjoyed great customer loyalty and produced something that people used every day. As author Robert Miles told *Chief Executive* magazine, Buffett "invests in companies like Gillette because he loves the fact that millions of men grow whiskers every night."

Nevertheless, not everyone was enamored of Buffett's deal with Gillette, or of his deal with Salomon Brothers. Some critics charged that Buffett used his purchases of convertible preferred stock to protect CEOs he liked. Owners of common stock—especially small investors—were the big losers in these arrangements, the critics charged. That is because share prices rise before a hostile takeover, but Buffett's huge investments made it impossible for Perelman to buy enough stock to engineer such a takeover.

Buffett saw things differently. The deals benefited his Berkshire Hathaway shareholders—who were, after all, his first concern. And because the convertible preferred stock had to be held for several years, the deals provided long-term stability for the companies in question.

Still, in the Salomon Brothers deal, Buffett ultimately got more than he had bargained for. Buffett had great faith in the ability of his friend John Gutfreund to manage Salomon and its more than 6,000 employees effectively and ethically. That faith, it turned out, was misplaced.

Gutfreund awarded large performance bonuses to his managers, even in years when the firm's profits stumbled and its stock stayed flat. Buffett found this unacceptable. He detested performance bonuses, feeling that a company's health rested in reinvestment of its profits, rather than in rewards for special members of its workforce.

One of Buffett's first actions upon assuming a seat on Salomon's board of directors was to demand that Gutfreund reduce the pool of executive bonus money. Under pressure from his colleagues, many of whom earned significant profits for Salomon, Gutfreund actually raised the bonuses. Then the Salomon Brothers firm became embroiled in a scandal that threatened to close it down, taking all of its stockholders' investments with it.

A thirty-four-year-old government bond trader with Salomon committed fraud by bidding for U.S. Treasury bonds on behalf of customer companies that had not authorized the bids. In this way the trader was able to purchase more bonds than Salomon would have legally been allowed to buy. The trader in question was allowed to operate with little oversight from Salomon, but some of his colleagues discovered the fraud nonetheless. They reported the activity to Gutfreund.

Gutfreund should have fired the trader and notified the U.S. Treasury Department immediately. He did neither. He decided to try to keep all news of the fraudulent deals inside the company. Gutfreund was afraid the bad press would hurt Salomon, which was already struggling to preserve its position in the stock and bond market.

The brazen trader, feeling that no one was watching, continued to buy bonds in the same manner until traders from other firms began to notice and complain. In May of 1991, agents of the U.S. Securities and Exchange Commission began to investigate Salomon. Even then Gutfreund did not confess his knowledge of his employee's misdeeds. A month later the federal government launched a full-fledged criminal probe of Salomon's bond-buying practices.

As news of the alleged illegal behavior spread, Salomon's stock price fell. Even after the trader under investigation was fired, questions remained about how much Gutfreund knew about the half-dozen illegal deals the trader had completed. Since the illegal practice involved the U.S. government, the Treasury Department threatened to expel Salomon from its list of trading partners. Private firms doing business with Salomon withdrew their accounts. No one wanted to be associated with a tarnished investment house.

Salomon's fortunes slid further when Gutfreund finally admitted that he knew about the illegal trading before the investigation began—and his inaction allowed the trader to continue the practice. It quickly became apparent that Gutfreund would have to resign. Even that would not restore Salomon's reputation, however. The company needed to find a chairman who could revive customers' faith in the firm. Even more important, Salomon needed a chief who would cooperate with all federal investigators and assure them that no more cheating would be tolerated.

In desperation, Salomon's management asked Buffett to become interim chairman of the company. It was against Buffett's nature to accept such a post. He had made a fortune by investing in well-run companies and buying companies outright, but the only outfit he wanted to run was Berkshire Hathaway. It was as if Mrs. B suddenly asked him to come to her furniture store and take over its day-to-day operations. Granted, Buffett had been spending more days away from Omaha as his holdings diversified and his reputation grew. Yet he still preferred his daily routine in the quiet atmosphere of Kiewit Plaza. Taking over at Salomon would require a lengthy stay in Manhattan, during which Buffett would have to answer to federal investigators, unhappy customers, and an anxious staff.

If Salomon Brothers closed, Berkshire Hathaway would lose money, but not enough to shake Berkshire's immense profitability. Salomon was just one of many holdings in the Berkshire fold. Buffett felt no financial obligation to bail it out on behalf of his Berkshire clients.

What mattered in the end was principle. As a member of Salomon's board of directors, Buffett felt a responsibility to Salomon shareholders. He also felt that the firm's breakup might affect his reputation as a financier, or at least make it appear that he trusted the wrong people.

The frugal Buffett had finally bought a private jet with Berkshire Hathaway funds. Jokingly, he called the jet *The Indefensible*. He boarded the jet in Omaha and flew to New York.

Upon arrival at Salomon's headquarters, Buffett met with Gutfreund and his top deputies, as well as other board members. All of them were certain that Salomon would fold. They expected to hear very soon that the federal government was dropping Salomon's trading rights. Even without that bombshell they could not hope to keep enough customers in order to cover the firm's short-term debts.

But Buffett assessed the situation and said, "This is only a temporary setback." Buffett had, after all, faced similar situations with American Express and GEICO and had pulled both companies back from the brink.

Buffett joined Gutfreund onstage in the company's auditorium while Gutfreund resigned. Knowing that his words would be repeated throughout the media, Buffett addressed the assembled Salomon managers seriously but optimistically. The firm would survive, he said, because unethical behavior would not be tolerated.

From mid-August 1991 until June of 1992, Buffett served as the interim chairman of Salomon Brothers. The period would be among the most stressful of his life. Within weeks of assuming the chairmanship he was called to Washington, D.C., to testify before the House Subcommittee on Banking and Finance. There he issued an apology on behalf of Salomon Brothers, admitting that an employee of the firm had committed a crime while others had covered it up. He appealed to the members of the subcommittee to allow Salomon to continue to trade with the Treasury Department. He concluded:

> I want [Salomon] employees to ask themselves whether they are willing to have any contemplated act appear on the front page of their local paper the next day, to be read by their spouses, children, and friends. . . . If they follow this test, they need not fear my other message to them: Lose money for the firm and I will be understanding; lose a shred of reputation for the firm, and I will be ruthless.

Buffett appears before a House Commerce subcommittee during his time as interim chairman of Salomon Brothers, Inc. *(Courtesy of AP Images/Marcy Nighswander)*

Buffett's testimony before Congress bought Salomon a reprieve. But months of difficult and sometimes frustrating work followed. Buffett demanded strict accounting from every department, a practice that had been lax during Gutfreund's term. He also cut the performance bonuses, telling managers who complained to find new jobs. Some of them did. Under his supervision, the workforce at Salomon dwindled, but by the end of 1991 the company had already begun to regain its reputation. Wall Street analysts attributed the company's survival to Buffett's calm handling of the crisis, his prior reputation for ethical behavior when he testified in Washington, and his cost-cutting efforts within the firm.

In June 1992, having succeeded in rescuing Salomon Brothers, Buffett left his post as interim chairman. He returned to Omaha. "You can tell from Berkshire's 1991–92 results that the company didn't miss me while I was gone," Buffett wrote in his 1992 letter to Berkshire Hathaway shareholders. "But the reverse isn't true: I missed Berkshire and am delighted to be back full-time. There is no job in the world that is more fun than running Berkshire and I count myself lucky to be where I am."

Nine

Painting with Dollars

During the 1990s Warren Buffett became more aggressive than ever in courting and buying whole companies. At the same time, he refused to invest at all in computer, software, or dot-com (Internet-based) enterprises, even though other investors were wildly enthusiastic about the technology sector.

Carpeting, bricks, furniture, public utilities, jewelry—whatever the business, Buffett maintained his philosophy of searching for great companies that produced goods and services people needed and that were led by energetic managers. While Wall Street traders invested heavily in the home computer industry, Buffett quietly sold stock and reinvested the profits in the mainstays of Berkshire's portfolio, especially insurance.

Buffett may have shunned computer stocks, but he found a new friend at the epicenter of that industry: Microsoft founder

Bill Gates. Their association began in 1991, when they met at a party given by Gates's mother. For his part, Gates had no interest in meeting Buffett, who is twenty-five years his senior. "I wasn't sure what I was going to talk to him about," Gates told interviewer Charlie Rose. "And I was very busy, but my mom had a great group of people coming out, including Kay Graham and Warren, and kind of insisted that I come out there. So I actually took a helicopter out thinking, 'OK, once I've done what my mom expects, a couple of hours, I'll be back to my work.' But then it was fantastic."

Buffett, on the other hand, had been eager to get to know the young giant in the computer field. "All my life I have been looking for somebody who didn't want to meet me," he joked.

Buffett and Gates spent several hours that night talking about what Buffett loved best—business. They also discovered a mutual fondness for bridge, and their friendship deepened as they began to play the card game online, Gates from Seattle and Buffett from Omaha.

Despite their friendship, Buffett never bought Microsoft stock for Berkshire Hathaway. Gates, on the other hand, bought Berkshire Hathaway stock for his personal portfolio.

During the summer of 1992 a single share of Berkshire stock hit $10,000. Ten months later it was trading at $17,800. In 1969, when Buffett took over the management of Berkshire full time, a share had cost just $43.

Most companies would have split the stock long before it had risen so far. In a stock split, each share becomes two shares, while the price per share typically drops by half. This means that while shareholders own twice as many shares, the total value of their investment remains the same. However,

Buffett and Bill Gates (right) playing a hand of bridge *(Courtesy of AP Images/Nati Harnik)*

the lower price per share makes the stock more affordable for new investors.

Buffett, however, never split Berkshire's stock. On several occasions he noted that part of the joy of his work was in seeing how high Berkshire stock could go. However, Buffett did make a concession to smaller investors. In 1996 he offered the less costly Berkshire Hathaway Class B stock. Its value would be one-thirtieth that of the full-priced Class A stock.

Like stock splits, Buffett also shunned dividends—annual checks to shareholders that reflect a percentage of a company's profits. Many investors like income from dividends, but Buffett always told his shareholders that he preferred to funnel annual profits back into additional profit-making enterprises under his supervision. If shareholders needed cash, they could always sell some of their Berkshire Hathaway stock.

Buffett's philosophy most benefited long-term investors in Berkshire Hathaway, many of whom became multimillionaires by virtue of the 20 percent average annual growth that Buffett achieved for his company's stock. The investor who made the most profit, however, was Buffett himself. He and his wife, Susie, owned more than one-third of the Class A shares.

Berkshire Hathaway's record of success—which continued year after year, regardless of how well or poorly the stock market as a whole performed—gave Buffett an aura of infallibility. Yet he did make his share of mistakes, which he quickly owned up to. For example, Buffett invested in USAir (now known as US Airways) right before the company entered a dismal business period, struggling with intense competition from other airlines, high employee compensation, and purchase and maintenance of its fleet. Buffett ultimately took a 75 percent loss on his USAir initial preferred stock.

Addressing USAir's disappointing performance in his 1994 letter to shareholders, Buffett wrote: "I correctly described this deal as an 'unforced error,' meaning that I was neither pushed into the investment nor misled by anyone when making it. Rather, this was a case of sloppy analysis, a lapse that may have been caused by the fact that we were buying a senior security or by hubris. Whatever the reason, the mistake was large."

The acquisition of three American shoe manufacturers—H. H. Brown, Lowell, and Dexter—proved similarly costly. In the early 1990s Berkshire acquired the companies at a total

USAir Chairman Stephen Wolf standing behind a model of a USAir jet. Buffett lost money by investing in USAir in the mid-1990s due to his "sloppy analysis" of the company. *(Courtesy of AP Images/Ed Bailey)*

cost of $650 million. By the end of the decade, profits on the shoe subsidiaries had declined by half as imported shoes flooded into the United States.

Yet another Buffett acquisition during the 1990s seemed ill advised (though it would eventually work out well). In 1998 Berkshire Hathaway bought General Re Corporation, a provider of reinsurance (insurance bought by other insurance companies to spread their risk). After it was brought under the Berkshire umbrella, General Re struggled.

In 1999 Berkshire Hathaway suffered its worst year during Warren Buffett's thirty-five-year tenure with the company. Per-share book value of Berkshire stock grew by a negligible 0.5 percent in 1999, even as the stock market as a whole boomed and the Standard & Poor 500 gained 21 percent.

Over the years, Buffett had consistently outperformed the S&P 500 and had presided over a 300,000 percent increase in the value of Berkshire stock. Yet he had steadfastly refused to invest in the technology-related and dot-com stocks that helped fuel the bull market of the 1990s. Buffett could not see the underlying value in these companies, and he was loath to invest in businesses he did not understand. Some Wall Street insiders claimed that Buffett simply did not understand the Internet-driven "new economy." They hinted that the Oracle of Omaha was washed up.

In early 2000, however, Buffett's misgivings about the technology sector were validated. As he had suspected, many computer-related companies turned out to be wildly overvalued, and their stock plummeted. Dot-coms went out of business by the dozens. While the overall stock market crashed, investors whose holdings were weighted toward the tech sector were hit especially hard.

Between 2000 and 2002, the S&P 500 lost about 40 percent of its value. Over the same period, Berkshire shareholders saw gains of more than 10 percent. Asked whether he had been irritated by the earlier suggestions that he was a has-been, Buffett replied, "Nothing bothers me like that. You can't do well in investments unless you think independently. And the truth is, you're neither right nor wrong because people agree with you. You're right because your facts and your reasoning are right. In the end that's all that counts."

If Buffett refused to follow the Wall Street herd, he also became a frequent critic of American corporate culture. Buffett has taken CEOs and their closest associates to task for enriching themselves at the expense of shareholders through bonuses, stock options, and extravagant retirement packages. "Too often, executive compensation in the U.S. is ridiculously out of line with performance," he wrote in a letter to his shareholders. "That won't change, moreover, because the deck is stacked against investors when it comes to the CEO's pay. The upshot is that a mediocre-or-worse CEO—aided by his handpicked VP of human relations and a consultant from the ever-accommodating firm of Ratchet, Ratchet, and Bingo—all too often receives gobs of money from an ill-designed compensation arrangement."

Buffett's many managers, from the presidents of See's Candies and Dairy Queen to the CEOs of General Re and Fruit of the Loom, receive generous salaries. However, they get no performance bonuses, special compensation plans, or options on Berkshire Hathaway stock. All net profits from every Berkshire-owned company become part of the pool of financial resources Buffett uses to invest as he and Charlie Munger see fit.

Buffett continued to invest heavily in acquiring new companies. He even began closing his annual letters to his shareholders with an open invitation to company owners to contact him if they wanted to work under the Berkshire umbrella. "If you have a business that fits, give me a call," one such letter concluded. "Like a hopeful teenage girl, I'll be waiting by the phone."

Jokes aside, Buffett did move quickly whenever he found a well-run firm he liked. That happened in 2002, when Doris Christopher, owner of the Pampered Chef, contacted him. In 1980, with an investment of just $3,000, Christopher had founded the business—which sells kitchen products, bakeware, and mixes for gourmet sauces and dips through home-demonstration parties. Twenty-two years later, the Pampered

Chef was generating annual sales of $700 million through a workforce of about 70,000 independent consultants working out of their homes.

True to form, Buffett studied the Pampered Chef's financial records closely. Then, in August, he invited Christopher and her CEO, Sheila O'Connell Cooper, to Omaha for a personal meeting. "I could tell that in a few minutes—and Doris could tell in a few minutes—that we were made for each other," Buffett told *Fortune* magazine. "I didn't know [the company's] name a few months ago, but I could tell that Doris and Sheila love running the business. . . . It's a better story than I am." By September Berkshire Hathaway's intention to acquire the Pampered Chef had been announced.

Doris Christopher fit the profile of a Berkshire manager: someone who shows the same kind of enthusiasm and work ethic that propels Buffett. Long after passing the age when most people retire, Buffett has continued to work, day after day, in the same modest office in Omaha's Kiewit Plaza that he has occupied for forty years. For the CEO of one of the world's most profitable companies, Buffett maintains a small corporate staff—fewer than twenty people work at Kiewit Plaza—and he pays himself only $100,000 per year, the same salary he has collected for twenty-five years.

"Why am I running down here every day and can hardly wait to get to work?" Buffett asked during a 2006 interview with Charlie Rose. "It isn't for the money. It's because I get to do my job the way I like to do it. I get to paint on my own canvas. I feel like I'm Michelangelo down here and I'm doing the Sistine Chapel. Now, nobody else may think so, but they don't say, use a little red paint instead of blue paint

Buffett wears an apron with the inscription "Berkshire Cooks!" at the Pampered Chef booth during the 2004 Berkshire Hathaway annual shareholders' meeting. *(Courtesy of AP Images/Nati Harnik)*

or something like that. I get to use whatever paint I want, paint whatever I want. I love it."

Work in Progress: A Profile of Berkshire Hathaway, 2006

Employees: 217,550
Assets: $248.437 billion
Revenues: $98.539 billion (33rd highest in world)
Profits: $11.015 billion (26th highest in world)

Milestone: On October 23, Berkshire Hathaway Class A became the first stock ever to close above $100,000 per share.

Sources: FORTUNE Global 500, July 23, 2007; MSNBC.com.

Buffett poses with a Berkshire Hathaway stock certificate. *(Courtesy of James Colburn/ZUMA Press)*

COMMON STOCK

No.BU236362

THIS CERTIFIES THAT

BERKSHIRE HATHAWAY INC.

TEN

The $37 Billion Gift

By law, every company that trades on the stock exchange must have an annual meeting that shareholders can attend. Berkshire Hathaway's annual meeting in Omaha is far more than a dry report of yearly earnings. It is a grand party that attracts shareholders from all parts of the world. Some come to celebrate their financial success, others to soak up the homespun wisdom of the man widely regarded as the world's greatest investor. Warren Buffett calls Berkshire's annual weekend gathering the "Woodstock of Capitalism," referring to the raucous rock concert held in New York State in 1969.

Buffett clearly enjoys these events and welcomes the opportunity to greet Berkshire shareholders. He makes no distinction between the ultra-wealthy owners of multiple Class A shares and the more ordinary investors who have bought a share or two of Class B stock. All are welcome to attend special parties (and buy deeply discounted goods) at local stores owned by Berkshire, such as the Nebraska Furniture Mart and Borsheim's, a jewelry store Buffett purchased in 1989. Those lucky enough to get a reservation—first come, first served—can dine with Buffett at Gorat's, his favorite Omaha steak house. Buffett mingles, shaking hands and signing autographs.

Berkshire's annual meeting has attracted as many as 27,000 people. The esteem in which Buffett is held sometimes approaches reverence. "Like every good Moslem goes to Mecca, I come here," a Belgian sports trainer told the *New York Times* during one gathering. "Every shareholder or capitalist should go one time or another to Omaha."

"It's a philosophy of investing and a philosophy of life," another shareholder said. "Buffett takes a very common-sense approach to life. You achieve what you achieve through hard work and sound management."

"This is a unique person in the history of capitalism," a Boston-based investor noted. "He's made most of us a lot of money."

The highlight of any Berkshire Hathaway annual meeting is the personal report delivered by Buffett and Charlie Munger. Hours before Buffett and Munger are scheduled to appear, shareholders begin lining up outside the arena where the event is held to get the best seats. When Buffett and Munger take the stage, they are greeted with the kind of loud, extended standing ovation usually reserved for superstar athletes.

The billionaire long ranked as the world's second-wealthiest person invariably demonstrates his self-effacing sense of

Buffett and Charlie Munger preside over a question and answer
session during Berkshire Hathaway's annual shareholders' meeting.
(Courtesy of AP Images/Nati Harnik)

humor and down-home charm. Throughout his presentation,
he trades jokes with the wisecracking Munger. He makes a
point of sipping Cokes and eating a treat from Dairy Queen,
and he urges the Berkshire faithful to buy the other products
that make their stock prices rise—GEICO insurance, Gillette
razors, Fruit of the Loom underwear.

In a question-and-answer session that can last up to six hours,
Buffett fields questions from the crowd. Topics might range
from the specifics of Berkshire's stock portfolio to Buffett's
views on CEO behavior, from how Berkshire Hathaway pays
its taxes to how globalization of the labor force has affected
the American economy. Buffett never dodges difficult questions, but he also declines to offer tips on stocks he thinks
will perform well over the next year. Instead he explains his

theories of value investment, his methods for judging talented managers, and his views on how national and international politics can influence the stock market. After the hours of questions, Buffett retires to Gorat's for a steak, just as he has for decades.

Around 1996, Buffett began to face a new question: Who would follow him as chairman of Berkshire after his death? At first Buffett joked that he intended to run the company from his grave since he enjoyed his work so much. But investors continued to be concerned that Buffett's abilities were unique, and that no one person would be able to fill his shoes.

In 1999 Buffett revealed how he expected a successor to run Berkshire. "I hope whoever follows me would behave pretty much as I would if I were to live forever," he declared. "I feel I owe it. I owe it to the people who sold me their businesses. They didn't have to sell to me. If I die tonight, I want them to get what they were expecting."

The following year Buffett revealed that he had discussed the question of a successor with his son Howard, a board member of Berkshire Hathaway. "I want Berkshire and the culture to continue, and [Howard] would be there to ensure that happens," Buffett said. "And he has my ideas about who I think should be running it."

Later Buffett indicated that Berkshire's board of directors had agreed on a successor who would step in immediately should Buffett die suddenly. Buffett did not name the individual but hinted that the person already worked among Berkshire's employees at Kiewit Plaza.

Buffett may have arranged for an orderly transition at Berkshire Hathaway, but he failed to make detailed plans for the dispersion of his vast personal fortune after his death. That is because he assumed his wife would be carrying out that task. However, Susie Buffett died suddenly of a stroke on July 29, 2004, while she and her husband were visiting friends in Cody, Wyoming.

Buffett's son, Howard Buffett *(Courtesy of AP Images/Nati Harnik)*

"Susie was two years younger than I, and women usually live longer than men," Buffett said in a *Fortune* magazine interview. "She and I always assumed that she would inherit my Berkshire stock and be the one who oversaw the distribution of our wealth to society, where both of us had always said it would go. And Susie would have enjoyed the process. . . . She would really have stepped on the gas."

Over the years, Warren Buffett had set up charitable foundations for his wife and each of his three children, allowing them to manage the funds and donate to causes they believed in. Howard, through his Howard Buffett Foundation, supports projects to increase crop production in Africa, wildlife conservation, and other environmental causes. Susan A. Buffett, Warren's daughter, heads a charity that funds early childhood education for low-income children, as well as public health initiatives. Warren's youngest son, Peter—a musician and composer—runs the Spirit Foundation, which issues grants in support of the arts, education, and human services.

However, Buffett's wife ran the largest of the family's charitable foundations. The Susan T. Buffett Foundation focused mainly on funding medical research and methods to curb population growth. It also supported hospices and other social services for the terminally ill.

After Susie's death, Buffett decided not to wait until his own passing to disperse his wealth. He considered donating his Berkshire stock to the Susan T. Buffett Foundation. But the foundation had only five employees, and Buffett was concerned that scaling it up to accept billions of dollars would overburden its administrator, his former son-in-law Allen Greenberg.

Buffett decided to give the bulk of his fortune to a foundation that was already scaled up. On June 26, 2006, he announced the phased donation of most of his Berkshire Hathaway stock to the Bill & Melinda Gates Foundation. At the time, the stock was worth some $31 billion. Buffett pledged an additional $6 billion in stock, to be divided among his family's four charitable foundations. The $37 billion gift was the largest charitable contribution in history.

In donating most of his fortune to the Bill & Melinda Gates Foundation, Buffett was applying to philanthropy principles he had successfully used in business. Like the presidents of companies Berkshire Hathaway buys, Melinda and Bill Gates—whom Buffett had known for fifteen years—demonstrated tremendous enthusiasm for their foundation, which focused on combating deadly diseases such as acquired immune deficiency syndrome (AIDS), malaria,

Bill Gates (left), Melinda Gates (middle), and Warren Buffett at the press conference held to announce Buffett's sizable donation to the Bill & Melinda Gates Foundation *(Courtesy of AP Images/Kristie Bull)*

and tuberculosis; global development; and education. With some $30 billion in pledges from the Gateses and others, it was already the largest private charitable foundation in the world. Its managers would be able to make effective use of Buffett's money.

"I'm getting two people enormously successful at something, where I've had a chance to see what they've done, where I know they will keep doing it—where they've done it with their own money, so they're not living in a fantasy world," Buffett said. "What can be more logical, in whatever you want done, than finding someone better equipped than you are to do it? Who wouldn't select Tiger Woods to take his place in a high-stakes golf game? That's how I feel about this decision about my money."

The Bill & Melinda Gates Foundation will benefit from Buffett's talent as well as his money: Buffett agreed to serve on the foundation's board of directors. He also planned to continue running Berkshire Hathaway. Because the Bill & Melinda Gates Foundation will receive Buffett's Berkshire stock in batches over time, and because it will not sell entire batches at once, the value of Buffett's gift will increase with any gains in Berkshire stock. If past performance is any guide, the foundation will likely receive considerably more than $31 billion from Warren Buffett. Berkshire Class A stock hit $100,000 per share in October 2006. A year later it was trading at around $128,000.

Only Buffett's extraordinary talent for investing and his incredible work ethic have made such success possible. When he is home in Omaha, Buffett continues to spend 85 percent of his waking hours reading, talking business on the telephone, or attending meetings.

Yet his life is not entirely controlled by his work. He loves to play bridge online with his sister and Bill Gates, among others. He has been known to share a round of golf with Tiger Woods. He has also lent his support to the political campaigns of politicians whose views he shares, including Arnold Schwarzenegger, California's Republican governor, and Senator Barack Obama, a Democratic candidate for president. When he held a board position with Capital Cities, he appeared on an ABC daytime drama, *All My Children*. He likes the stage as well. Once he played Daddy Warbucks in an Omaha community theater production of *Annie*.

On his seventy-sixth birthday, Buffett married his long-time companion Astrid Menks in a fifteen-minute civil ceremony held at his daughter Susie's home in Omaha. The couple continues to live in the home on Farnham Street that Buffett bought in 1958.

Buffett has declared his intention to work "until I lose my marbles." After more than a half-century as a full-time investor, he still relishes the challenge of finding undervalued stocks and well-run businesses to buy. He also clearly enjoys his ongoing partnership with Charlie Munger, whom Buffett describes as "the best partner a guy could have."

"It doesn't get any better than this," Buffett said of his life and career. "I mean, I don't know how long you can do it, but you're just plain lucky in life if you get to do something that you love doing with people that you love being around."

Timeline

1930   Born on August 30 in Omaha, Nebraska.

1943   With family, moves to Washington, D.C., after father is elected to U.S. House of Representatives.

1950   Earns bachelor's degree in business from the University of Nebraska, Lincoln; begins graduate school at Columbia University.

1951   Makes first purchase of GEICO stock; after earning master's degree, returns to Omaha and joins father's investment firm.

1952   Marries Susan Thompson.

1953   Daughter Susie born.

1954   Moves to New York to join firm of Graham-Newman; son Howard born.

1955   Returns to Omaha; creates investment partnership Buffett Associates Ltd.

1958   Son Peter is born.

1959   Meets Charlie Munger, who becomes
        business adviser and vice chairman of Berkshire
        Hathaway.

1962   Moves office from home to downtown Omaha
        high-rise, Kiewit Plaza; begins to buy stock
        in Berkshire Hathaway.

1963   Investment in American Express helps the
        company avoid bankruptcy after a scandal.

1965   Invests in the Walt Disney Company; takes
        control of Berkshire Hathaway.

1967   Net worth tops $10 million as his investment
        partnership grows to $67 million.

1968   Folds his investment partnership; retains
        Berkshire Hathaway.

1972   Buffett and Munger, with funds from Blue Chip
        Stamps, buys See's Candies.

1973   Joins the board of directors of The Washington
        Post Company.

1976   Begins the acquisition of GEICO insurance.

1977   Buys the *Buffalo Evening News*; wife,
        Susie, leaves Omaha to live in San Francisco but
        does not seek divorce.

1983	Buys the Nebraska Furniture Mart.
1984	Invests $500 million in Capital Cities/ABC; engineers a Berkshire takeover of Scott Fetzer Company.
1988	Buys $1 billion worth of Coca-Cola stock; buys a controlling interest in Salomon Brothers.
1989	Adds the Gillette Company to Berkshire's portfolio.
1991	Becomes interim chairman of Salomon Brothers; helps the company recover from a scandal involving illegal trading.
1993	Named wealthiest man in America by *Forbes* magazine as Berkshire Hathaway Class A stocks trade at more than $17,000 per share.
1994	Microsoft founder Bill Gates surpasses Buffett as the wealthiest person in the world.
1998	Acquires General Re and Dairy Queen.
1999	Berkshire Hathaway suffers its worst year ever during the boom in computer and tech stocks.
2000	Refusal to buy tech stocks vindicated when that sector of the market crashes.

2002   Buys Fruit of the Loom and the Pampered
        Chef.

2004   Susan Thompson Buffett dies of a stroke
        in Wyoming.

2006   Announces the donation of most of his
        personal fortune to the Bill & Melinda Gates
        Foundation; marries longtime companion
        Astrid Menks; Berkshire Hathaway Class A
        stock trades at more than $100,000 per share.

Sources

CHAPTER ONE: The Boy Businessman

p. 12, "the evil wedge . . ." Steve Jordon, "Partners Recall Grocery Days," *Omaha World-Herald*, May 5, 2006.

p. 14, "If I gave him ten . . ." Roger Lowenstein, *Buffett: The Making of an American Capitalist* (New York: Random House, 1995), 3.

p. 15, "I used to chart . . ." L. J. Davis, "Buffett Takes Stock," *New York Times*, April 1, 1990.

p. 16, "If I could be . . ." Warren Buffett, interview by Charlie Rose, *Charlie Rose Show,* PBS, July 10, 2006.

p. 17, "He was such . . ." Davis, "Buffett Takes Stock."

p. 17, "I told my parents . . ." Ibid.

CHAPTER TWO: A Capital Education

p. 22, "The barbershop operators . . ." Lowenstein, *Buffett*, 25.

p. 23, "I thought I would . . ." Davis, "Buffett Takes Stock."

p. 23, "fastening the chains . . ." Bill Kauffman, "Meet Warren Buffett's Daddy," *American Enterprise*, July–August, 2003.

p. 23, "Didn't change my . . ." Buffett, interview by Charlie Rose.

p. 24, "Likes math . . . a future stockbroker," Lowenstein, *Buffett,* 28.

p. 26-27, "The interview in Chicago . . ." Davis, "Buffett Takes Stock."

CHAPTER THREE: Ben's Bargains

p. 32, "Ben just says . . ." Buffett, interview by Charlie Rose.

p. 36, "I think it's a saner . . ." Davis, "Buffett Takes Stock."

p. 42, "Money won't make . . ." Janet Lowe, *Benjamin Graham on Value Investing: Lessons from the Dean of Wall Street* (Chicago: Dearborn Financial Publishing, 1994), 169.

CHAPTER FOUR: The Partnership

p. 43-44, "I didn't know . . ." Buffett, interview by Charlie Rose.

p. 54, "Such results should be . . ." Lowenstein, *Buffett,* 93.

CHAPTER FIVE: A New Direction

p. 57-58, "I am not attuned . . ." Mark Tier, *The Winning Investment Habits of Warren Buffett and George Soros* (New York: St. Martin's Press, 2005), 135.

p. 62, "I'll take the cash," Lowenstein, *Buffett,* 188.

CHAPTER SIX: Showdown in Buffalo

p. 71, "Although our profit margins . . ." Warren Buffett, chairman's letter to Berkshire Hathaway shareholders (1983), http://www.berkshirehathaway.com/letters/1983.html (accessed October 2, 2007).

p. 71, "Susie was the sun . . ." Lowenstein, *Buffett,* 227.

p. 72, "I really like my life . . ." Ibid., 230.

CHAPTER SEVEN: The Oracle of Omaha

p. 74, "What I must understand . . ." Anthony Bianco, "The Warren Buffett You Don't Know," *BusinessWeek. com*, July 5, 1999. http://www.businessweek.com/ datedtoc/1999/9927.htm (accessed October 18, 2007).

p. 76, "I'd rather wrestle grizzlies . . ." Buffett, chairman's letter (1983).

p. 77, "I . . . feel it inappropriate . . ." Warren Buffett, chairman's letter to Berkshire Hathaway shareholders (1985), http://www.berkshirehathaway.com/ letters/1985.html (accessed October 17, 2007).

p. 77, "Should you find yourself . . ." Buffett, chairman's letter (1985).

p. 79, "We should note . . ." Warren Buffett, chairman's letter to Berkshire Hathaway shareholders (1986), http:// www.berkshirehathaway.com/letters/1986.html (accessed October 17, 2007).

CHAPTER EIGHT: For the Love of Cherry Coke

p. 87, "There just comes a point . . ." Warren Buffett, interview by Charlie Rose, *Charlie Rose Show,* PBS, July 11, 2006.

p. 89, "invests in companies like Gillette . . ." Russ Banham, "The Warren Buffett School," *Chief Executive*, December 1, 2002.

p. 92, "This is only a temporary . . ." Lowenstein, *Buffett,* 382.

p. 93, "I want [Salomon] employees . . ." Ibid., 395.

p. 94, "You can tell . . ." Warren Buffett, chairman's letter to Berkshire Hathaway shareholders (1992), http://www.

berkshirehathaway.com/letters/1992.html (accessed
October 17, 2007).

CHAPTER NINE: Painting with Dollars

p. 96, "I wasn't sure . . ." Bill Gates, interview by
Charlie Rose, *Charlie Rose Show,* PBS, July 12, 2006.

p. 96, "All my life . . ." Warren Buffet, interview by
Charlie Rose, *Charlie Rose Show,* PBS, July 12, 2006.

p. 98, "I correctly described . . ." Warren Buffett,
chairman's letter to Berkshire Hathaway shareholders
(1994), http://www.berkshirehathaway.com/letters/1994.
html (accessed October 18, 2007).

p. 100, "Nothing bothers me . . ." Julia Boorstin, "The
Oracle of Everything," *Fortune*, November 11, 2002.

p. 101, "Too often, executive compensation . . ." Warren
Buffett, chairman's letter to Berkshire Hathaway
shareholders (2005), http://www.berkshirehathaway.
com/letters/2005ltr.pdf (accessed October 18, 2007).

p. 101, "If you have a business . . ." Ibid.

p. 102, "I could tell . . ." Boorstin, "Oracle."

p. 102,104, "Why am I running . . ." Buffett, interview with
Charlie Rose, July 11, 2006.

CHAPTER TEN: The $37 Billion Gift

p. 107, "Like every good . . ." David Barboza, "A
Capitalist Hero Keeps on Pitching," *New York Times*,
May 9, 1999.

p. 107, "It's a philosophy . . ." Ibid.

p. 107, "This is a unique person . . ." Ibid.

p. 109, "I hope whoever follows . . ." Bianco, "The
Warren Buffett You Don't Know."

p. 109, "I want Berkshire . . ." David Barboza, "Taking After
His Father, Sort Of," *New York Times*, September 3, 2000.

p. 110, "Susie was two years . . ." Carol J. Loomis, "A Conversation with Warren Buffett," *Fortune*, June 25, 2006.

p. 112-113, "I'm getting two people . . ." Ibid.

p. 114, "until I lose my marbles," Buffett, interview by Charlie Rose, July 11, 2006.

p. 114, "the best partner . . ." Ibid.

p. 114, "It doesn't get any better . . ." Buffett, interview by Charlie Rose, July 10, 2006.

Bibliography

Altucher, James. *Trade Like Warren Buffett.* New York: John Wiley, 2005.

Christopher, Doris. *The Pampered Chef: The Story Behind the Creation of One of America's Most Beloved Companies.* New York: Random House, 2005.

Graham, Katharine. *Personal History.* New York: Alfred A. Knopf, 1997.

Hagstrom, Robert G. *The Essential Buffett: Timeless Principles for the New Economy.* New York: John Wiley, 2001.

_____. *The Warren Buffett Way: Investment Strategies of the World's Greatest Investor.* New York: John Wiley, 1994.

Kilpatrick, Andrew. *Of Permanent Value: The Story of Warren Buffett.* New York: McGraw-Hill, 1998.

Lowe, Janet. *Benjamin Graham on Value Investing: Lessons from the Dean of Wall Street.* Chicago: Dearborn Financial Publishing, 1994.

_____. *Warren Buffett Speaks: Wit and Wisdom from the World's Greatest Investor.* New York: John Wiley, 1997.

Lowenstein, Roger. *Buffett: The Making of an American Capitalist.* New York: Random House, 1995.

Malkiel, Burton G. *A Random Walk Down Wall Street.*
New York: W.W. Norton, 1991.

Morio, Ayano. *Warren Buffett: An Illustrated Biography of
the World's Most Famous Investor.* New York: John
Wiley, 2004.

Pendergrast, Mark. *For God, Country and Coca-Cola:
The Unauthorized History of the Great American
Soft Drink and the Company That Makes It.* New
York: Scribner's, 1993.

Steele, Jay. *Warren Buffett: Master of the Market.* New
York: Avon Books, 1999.

Web sites

http://www.berkshirehathaway.com
The official home page of Berkshire Hathaway Inc. contains links to annual reports, company news releases, Warren Buffett's letters to shareholders, and other information.

http://money.cnn.com/2006/06/25/magazines/fortune/charity2.fortune/index.htm
A *Fortune* magazine editor's conversation with Warren Buffett about his ideas on philanthropy and his decision to give most of his money to the Bill & Melinda Gates Foundation.

Index